MICHELLE
SWEENEY

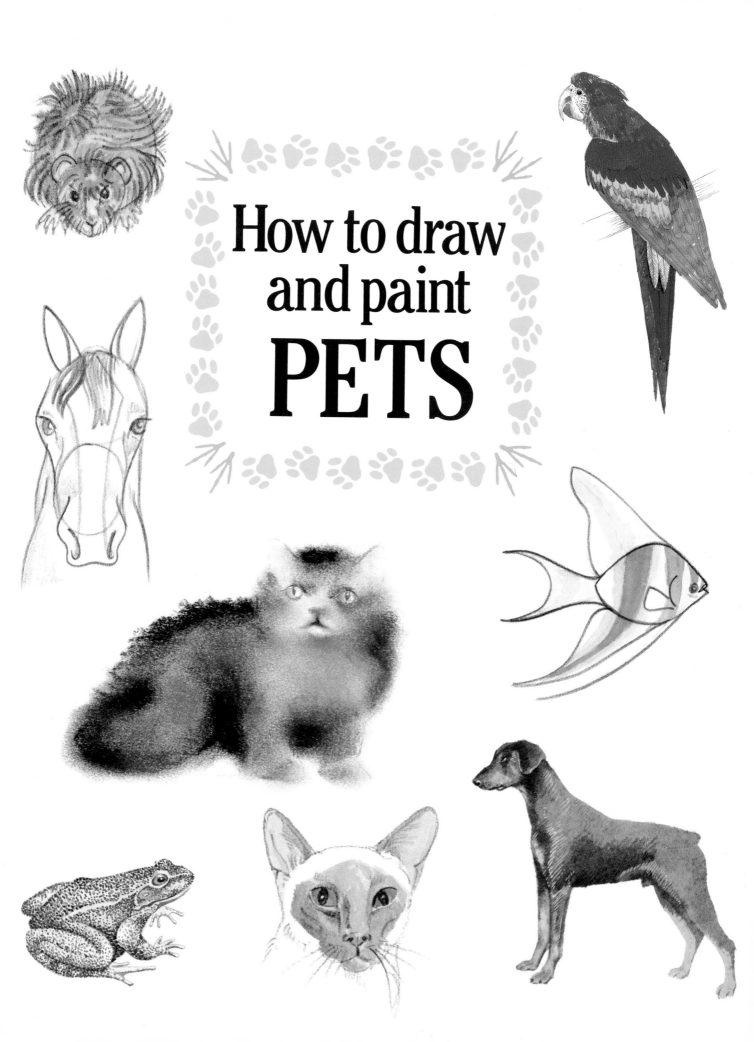

How to draw and paint
PETS

How to draw and paint
PETS

DIANA CRAIG

THE WELLFLEET PRESS
WELLFLEET

A QUARTO BOOK

Published by Wellfleet Press
110 Enterprise Avenue
Secaucus, New Jersey 07094

ISBN 1-55521-716-8

Reprinted 1993

This book was designed and produced by Quarto Publishing plc,
The Old Brewery, 6 Blundell Street, London N7 9BH

Designers Hazel Edington, Penny Dawes
Assistant art director Chloë Alexander
Project editor Helen Douglas-Cooper
Senior editor Kate Kirby
Artists Sally Launder, Vana Haggerty, Kevin Maddison, David Kemp,
Kate Gwynn, Neal Cobourne
Photographer Martin Norris

Art director Moira Clinch
Publishing director Janet Slingsby

With thanks to the Canonbury Art Shop, London
Typeset by ABC Typesetting Limited, Bournemouth
Manufactured in Singapore by Eray Scan Pte Ltd
Printed in Singapore by Star Standard Industries Pte. Ltd.

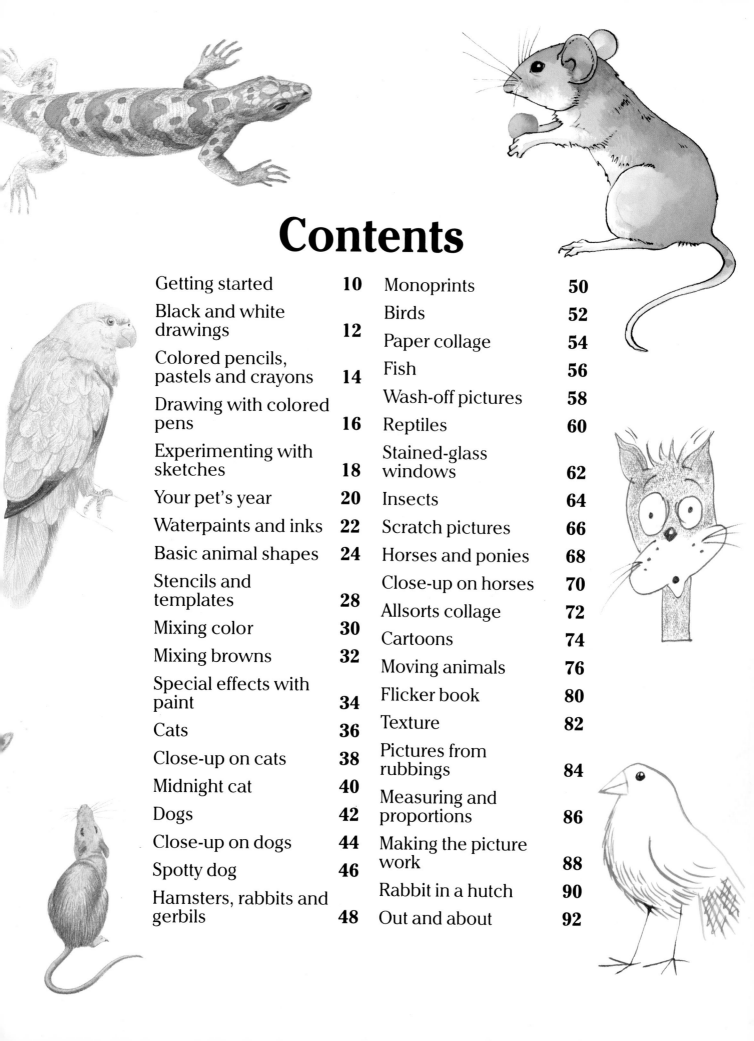

Contents

Getting started

Before you start to work, you should get together all the things you will need – then you can enjoy making your pictures without having to stop to find something you've forgotten. But first, have a look through this book. It may give you some new ideas for different materials and tools to try out.

A place to work

Where you work will depend on what materials you are using. You can draw in a hardcover sketchbook almost anywhere, but if you are using a loose sheet of paper you will need a firm surface to work on. A tabletop will do, but fixing your paper to a drawing board is even better because it keeps the paper firmly in place. You can buy ready-made boards, or make your own from chipboard or plywood. Fix your paper to the board with paper clips or thumbtacks.

Brushes

The better your brushes, the better the results they will give – and the easier they will be to use. The brushes that come in paint sets are thin and floppy and it is very hard to control them properly. You can buy good-quality brushes in art stores. Nylon and bristle brushes are not too expensive. Nylon is soft and good for thin paint such as **watercolor**. Bristle is stiffer and good for thicker paint such as **poster paint**. For painting details, you will need a small, pointed nylon brush, and one or two larger brushes, either nylon or bristle, for painting bigger areas.

Paper

There are all kinds of paper for different uses. Drawing paper has a smooth surface that is good for pencil drawing. Rougher and softer paper is good for **pastels** or **powder paints. Watercolors** contain a lot of water, so they need a thick paper that does not wrinkle too much. It's a

The best place to store all your materials safely is in a cupboard. Drawing pads and paper can be stored flat, and you can organize your things so that you can find what you need quickly. It will also give you somewhere to keep, or display, the work you have done.

good idea to have a small sketchbook to carry around with you so that you can do sketches whenever you want.

Palettes

It isn't necessary to have a real artist's palette for mixing up your colors. You can use an old plate or small tray. An old muffin tin is also useful because you can mix good quantities of different color in each of the hollows.

Water pots

Use a sturdy container to keep water in, or it may fall over. A clean glass jar or an old saucepan is ideal. Make sure it is not too small, or the water will quickly get dirty and spoil your colors, and remember to change the water frequently. Keep your water container away from the edge of your work surface, on your right side if you are right-handed and on your left if you are left-handed – that way, you are less likely to knock it over.

Keep it clean

Covering your clothes and your work surface will protect them from marks and stains that might not wash off. Wear an apron or old shirt to protect your clothes, and cover your work surface with newspaper.

Look after it

If you look after your materials, they will last much longer and be easier to use. Always wash your brushes after use, or old paint will clog the hairs and make the brushes hard. After painting, rinse brushes out in cold or lukewarm water (hot water melts the glue that holds the hairs in place). Then wash them gently with soap or dishwashing detergent, and finally rinse them clean. Store your brushes in jars with the heads upward. Always remember to put the tops back on paint pots and felt-tip pens, too, or they will dry out.

Save it

Keep a lookout for anything that you think might be useful, and save it! The backs of old business letters can be used for painting pictures as they are often written on good, thick paper (but check that nobody needs them first). Old jars can be used for holding water, and plastic cups can be used for mixing paint in (make sure they are not too light, or they may fall over). And of course any small objects, such as buttons, scraps of wrapping paper or foil, cotton, twigs, pasta shapes, or pictures cut from old magazines, are ideal for making collages.

Black and white drawings

Different drawing materials make different marks. Generally, soft materials such as crayon or pastel look rough and smudgy; harder ones such as pencil or ballpoint pen make thinner, neater marks and lines. Try them out and choose the best ones for your picture.

Charcoal is good for big, quick drawings, but it can get messy and is not so good for details. If you want to do a detailed picture, try pen and ink. Thin felt-tip pen is also good for neat lines; thick felt-tip is best for wide lines or marks, or filling in.

Experiment with how you use your materials – drawing in smooth, even lines isn't the only way to make a picture. Try scribbling to show, say, a shaggy coat, or use zigzag lines for the scales on a fish or lizard. Or you could build up your picture with lots of little dots and short lines, or crisscrossing lines (this is called *cross-hatching*): the more crisscrossing lines you do, the darker your picture will be. Smudge or rub out part of your picture and see what that looks like.

Hard pencils make thin, neat, light lines. Hard pencils are marked "H," with a number. The higher the number, the harder the pencil.

Soft pencils make wider, softer, darker lines. They are marked "B," with a number. The higher the number, the softer the pencil. (Medium pencils are marked "HB" or "F.")

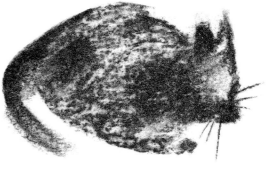

Charcoal makes wide, "rough" lines, and smudges easily.

Chalks give a nice crumbly line, and are perfect for filling in.

Thick felt-tip pens can make broad lines or dots, and are good for filling in.

Thin felt-tip pens make an even line. They are available with very fine points for detailed drawing.

Pen and ink makes a strong, black line.

What shall I use for cats?

Choose the drawing material that will look most like your pet. For a cat with short fur, lots of little lines in thin felt-tip pen could look like individual hairs, and you could fill in with thicker pen if you liked. If your cat is fluffy, a smudgy material like pastel or charcoal would be good.

Patch says... You can make symmetrical shapes, such as a butterfly, by putting an ink blob on paper and folding it over.

Lydia used soft pencil to draw her rabbit. See how she has used the pencil to show the way the fur grows.

Cheryl chose black felt-tip pen to draw a simple outline of her dog and for filling in the details.

13

Colored pencils, pastels, and crayons

There are many wonderful colored drawing materials to choose from, all with their own special qualities.

You have probably already used colored pencils. Their sharp points are good for drawing details, and if you press lightly, you can also color in bigger areas. They make soft, delicate pictures. But did you know that you can also "paint" with certain pencils and crayons? Watercolor pencils and crayons are just like ordinary colored pencils except that, if you paint over them with water, the color spreads like paint.

Pastels and oil pastels all make similar marks. Pastels are soft and smudge easily, so you can blend colors by rubbing them with your finger or a piece of absorbent cotton. Oil pastels give stronger colors, and won't smudge.

If you have used ordinary pastels for your picture, be especially careful with it when you have finished. Hold the paper by the edges or it may smudge.

Wax crayons won't smudge and you can't rub them out, but you can "blend" colors by putting one on top of another – some of the color beneath will show through.

colored pencil

watercolor pencil

pastels, chalks (use their ends to draw with: hold them on their sides to color in)

oil pastel

wax crayon

Making highlights

Eyes and noses will look much more real if you give them highlights to make them look shiny.

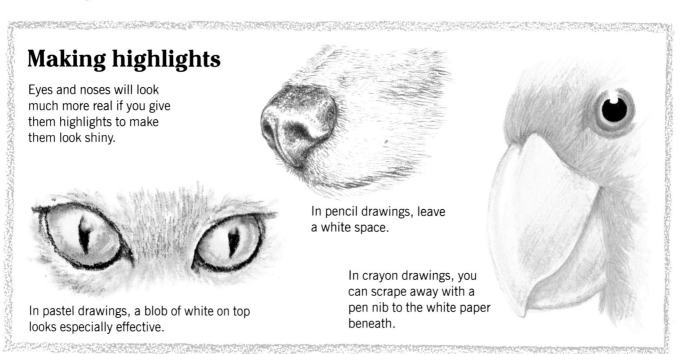

In pencil drawings, leave a white space.

In pastel drawings, a blob of white on top looks especially effective.

In crayon drawings, you can scrape away with a pen nib to the white paper beneath.

Patch says... Look carefully to see how many different colors there are on your pet. There may be subtle changes of color that you haven't yet noticed – say, around its nose, or on its paws.

Rabbit in pastels
This picture was done in pastels, on special pastel paper (you can use any slightly rough paper instead). See how the pastel has been lightly smudged to blend the colors. Using the colored paper makes the picture more interesting, and you can allow some of the paper color to show through.

Rabbit in colored pencil Another picture of the same rabbit was done with colored pencil. Here, the pencil has been used to color in lots of short lines to look like the rabbit's fur. See how the lines change direction, just like fur. Colored pencil drawings stand out best on white paper.

Drawing with colored pens

F elt-tip pens are very different from colored pencil or pastel, so you should not try to use them in the same way. They make much stronger lines and marks, so they are not suitable for soft, delicate pictures. To get the best from felt-tips, the trick is to work boldly!

Another difference is that felt-tip pen marks cannot be rubbed out, but don't be afraid of making mistakes. A slightly "wrong" outline will just make your picture look more unusual and interesting – or you can draw over the line again, and this will also add interest. Remember that the more practice you have, the more confident you will become.

You can also do colored drawings with ballpoint pens and old-fashioned "dip" pens, but they both have disadvantages. Ballpoints come in so few colors that your drawing would not look very exciting, and it is somewhat of a waste to use colored ink just to draw fine lines or dots. The colors are so rich and beautiful you would enjoy them much more if you painted them on with a brush, in broad strokes, so you could really *see* them.

Big, round felt-tip pens make broad lines and dots.

Wedge-tip marker pens give bold, even lines.

Dip pens can make bold or spidery lines, depending on how hard you press.

Fine felt-tip pens make even, fine lines.

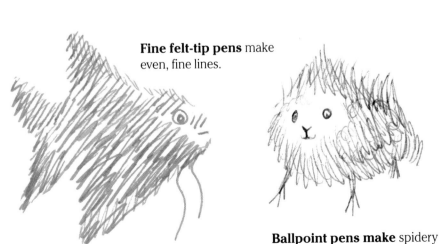

Ballpoint pens make spidery lines – but keep the tip clean or the ink may blob.

Fountain pens give a clean, strong line.

Thin felt-tip was used on the head.

Parrot from colored pens This beautiful, bold parrot was done with different kinds of pen.

Dip pen was used for the beak and the outlines of the feathers.

Broad felt-tip pen was used to color in the main areas.

Ballpoint pen was used for the front neck feathers, and for the perch.

Felt-tip pen effects

If you want a softer effect with felt-tip pens, try applying the color in lots of tiny lines or dots. This technique is called *pointillism.* When you hold your picture at a distance away from you, the dots will "blend" to make a different color.

Experimenting with sketches

Sketching does not only mean doing quick pencil drawings in your sketchbook. Experiment with all kinds of drawing materials. See what happens if you paint a watercolor wash over a pencil sketch (a "wash" is a transparent layer of paint which has been mixed with water to make it thinner). Or try drawing with a watercolor pencil and then painting over it with water to make the colors run.

Experiment with wax crayons. What happens if you draw with different colors on top of each other?

Wax crayons are greasy, and grease and water don't mix, so what happens if you paint watercolor over your crayon sketch? Is it the same if you paint on the watercolor first?

Make notes about what you have done. Label each sketch with the materials you used, and which you used first. If you think a particular material would be really good for doing, say, an animal's fur, write this down too. For example, smudged gray, black, or orange pastel may really look like fluffy cat's fur.

What other experiments can you think of?

Wax crayon and wash First the outline and main details were drawn with crayon.

Next, some of the fur was colored in using yellow for the light areas and gray and purple for the dark areas.

Last, a watercolor wash was painted over, leaving some areas white to create highlights.

Watercolor pencil was used to draw the outline and main details of this guinea pig.

Some shading was added in the ears and below the body.

Water was painted over to make the pencil run, like paint. See how this has created darker areas.

18

"Ideas scrapbook"

As well as experimenting with materials, why not also use your sketchbook as an "ideas scrapbook"? Whenever you find a picture of a pet animal you like, cut it out and stick it in your sketchbook. You can simply copy the picture, or use it to develop some ideas of your own.

Here are some of the places you may find pictures of pet animals for your "scrapbook" (but make sure no one else needs them before you cut them up).

- photos
- stamps
- magazine advertisements
- cards
- labels from cans or packages of pet food
- scraps of wrapping paper

Patch says... Why not do drawings of the same animal using different materials? Look at the effect each one has, and compare them to see which one is best for your pet.

Types of fur and feathers Think of all the different kinds of fur animals have – some is short, straight, and smooth, some is long and curly. Experiment in your sketchbook to get the look of different fur. Make studies of the different shapes and textures of feathers in the same way.

19

Your pet's year

Your sketchbook is one of the most important tools you have. The more you use it, the better your drawing will become, and the more you will have learned about the different materials you have experimented with. But there is another way in which your sketchbook is very useful. As you keep doing drawings of your pet – sleeping, eating, playing, and so on – just think of what a wonderful record you are building up of all the things your pet does.

Why not put all these pictures together to make a really special record of your pet's life, such as an "all-seasons poster" or a calendar of your pet's year. You can either use the sketches you already have, do one specially for each season or month, or do more finished pictures based on your original sketches.

You will need
- 12 pictures of your pet (one for each month)
- 12 pieces of paper
- calendar for next year
- stapler
- glue
- scissors
- paper punch (if available)
- cord or wool for hanging your calendar

1

All-seasons poster For this you will need four different pictures of your pet, one for each season. For example, you could have your dog with flowers for spring; sleeping in the sun for summer; chasing leaves for fall; and in a cozy basket or by the fire for winter. Paste your pictures on a large piece of paper, writing the name of the season below.

Pet calendar On each sheet of paper, paste the picture for that month and the right sheet from the calendar.

20

2

3

1991 **AUGUST** 1991

Sun	Mon	Tu	Wed	Th	Fri	Sat
-	-	-	-	1	2	3
4	5	6	7	8	9	10
11	12	13	14	15	16	17
18	19	20	21	22	23	24
25	26	27	28	29	30	31

Staple the sheets together and make two holes at the top with scissors or a paper punch (you may need an adult's help).

Thread the cord or wool through the holes and knot it. Then hang up your calendar.

21

Paints and inks

There are three basic kinds of water-based paint: *gouache*, *watercolor* and *acrylics*. They are called "water-based" because you can mix them with water.

All these paints are made of a colored powder, called *pigment*, mixed with something to bind them together. Watercolors and gouache are mixed with gum, and acrylics are mixed with a chemical binder.

Water paints come in two qualities: students' and artists'. Students' paints are cheaper than artists', but they contain less pigment so the colors are not as strong.

You can also paint pictures with colored inks. Inks and the different paints all have their own special qualities. Which you choose will depend on the kind of picture you want to paint, and how much money you want to spend.

Gouache comes in two forms, poster paint and designers' gouache. It is thicker than watercolor, and it doesn't let the paper show through. It can be watered down easily, but will pick up the color underneath if it is very watery. Work the colors and tones into or over each other.

Acrylics come in tubes or jars. They can be applied with a dry brush, like the mouse below right, or applied watered down, one color over another in layers.

Watercolor is a thin, watery paint that comes in tubes or blocks, called pans. Because it is transparent, the colors show up best on white paper. It should be used on stretched paper or thick watercolor paper, or card. Build up layers of color and tone, but be careful not to overwork the painting.

Stippling with gouache

Stippling is a good technique to use with paint like gouache, which dries to a flat finish. "Stippling" means to apply paint in lots of dots or little lines. It's another way of mixing a color. Instead of mixing it up from other colors and then painting it on, you "mix" it by applying the different colors to the paper.

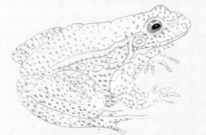

First draw the outline, and brush over a light wash of color, leaving the highlights white. Apply dots of the main color all over.

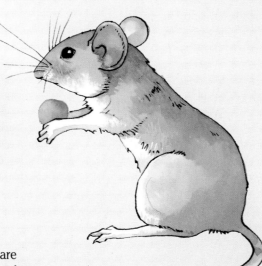

Add dots of lighter and darker colors to create light and dark areas. For the frog, permanent green, sky blue, burnt umber and orange lake light were used.

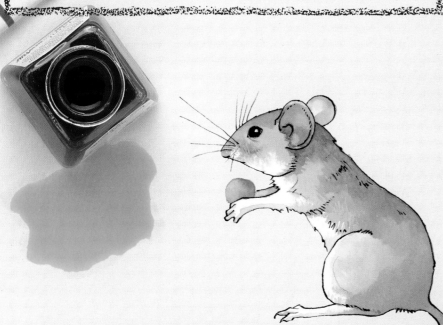

Individual dots of color combine to create an overall effect of color and tone.

Patch says...
You can lift off watercolor while it is still wet to make highlights. Before the paint dries, quickly brush over it with a dry brush, or take the paint off with a dry tissue or cloth.

A watercolor cat Watercolor can be used to create a soft effect by brushing the color on to wet paper.

1 Lightly draw the animal's outline with pencil.

2 Paint all over the shape with clean water, going slightly beyond the edge. Leave the water to soak in.

3 Apply thin washes of color to the wet paper, stopping before you get to the edge. Use stronger color to build up detail.

Inks come in bottles. They are slightly transparent, but the colors are quite strong. You can mix the colors in the same way as for paints, and water them down if the color is too strong. You can put layers over each other.

23

Basic animal shapes

One of the main things that makes one kind of animal look different from another is the shape of its body. A clever trick to make drawing an animal easier is first to divide its body up into a few simple shapes, such as circles, triangles, and rectangles.

For example, if you are drawing a cat sitting facing you, you could do a circle for the head and a triangle for the body. If you are drawing a small dog from the side, you could do three rectangles of different sizes for the head, neck, and body.

On these pages we have made it even simpler by using nothing but circles and ovals. Have a look at the drawings to see how to turn these basic shapes into pictures of real animals.

Cats Here is a picture of a cat sitting down, viewed from the side. What shapes can you see in its body?

Here is a drawing of the same cat, broken down into simple shapes. Make sure that the shapes are the right size – for example, the head should not be too big compared to the body.

When you are happy with your rough drawing, draw an outline around the edge. Rub out any lines that you no longer need, but leave important ones such as the line of the chin.

Fill in the silhouette with color, adding details such as eyes and whiskers.

Sitting dog This dog has a fairly long neck, so the circles are some way apart.

Now that the fur has been colored in, the dog looks very realistic.

A dog begging is a little more complicated, but you can still see the circles and

oval shapes. Make sure you get the shapes of the nose and eye right.

Rabbits (side view)
These are easy to draw because they are made up of lots of simple, rounded shapes.

They have short necks, so the circle for the head overlaps the oval shape.

Rabbits (front view)
Because it's seen from a slight angle, the circle for the head is not quite in the middle of the body.

Little details such as the turned-over ear tips make it look like a real animal.

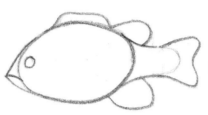

Front view of fish The fish has a very narrow body, so the oval shape is thin.

Make sure the fins are even, or the fish will look lopsided.

Fish from the side makes a bigger, wider oval.

You don't have to draw every single scale to make the fish look real.

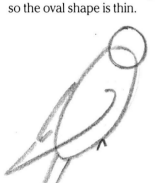

Budgerigars are tricky, but they still fit into circles and ovals.

Don't try to paint every feather or you will get into a muddle.

Parrots have stubby tails, and are larger than budgerigars.

Like all birds, parrots have beady eyes.

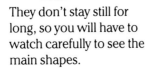

Lizards have long bodies, so the oval shape is very stretched out.

They don't stay still for long, so you will have to watch carefully to see the main shapes.

Lizard from the front
The head is a circle with a triangle below.

The body looks round because it's seen from the front. This is called foreshortening.

For the side view of a pony, start like this.

Then color it in.

Pony (front view) The front view makes even easier shapes.

Don't forget the forelock when you color in.

Pony's head from side A pony's head is a little more difficult.

You will have to use triangles as well as ovals.

Pony's head from front A pony's head is fairly long, and broad at the top.

The eyes bulge out slightly, and the ears are pointed.

Guinea pig (front view) Use round shapes; the ears are half circles.

It's best to draw the shapes before you put in the fur.

Guinea pig (side view) From the side, you can see how big guinea pigs' heads are.

Does your guinea pig have long hair or short hair?

Turtle from front Turtles have big oval-shaped shells...

...and scaly, rectangular legs.

Turtle from side Turtles' necks look fairly long.

They have lovely patterns on their shells.

Mouse from side Mice are easy to draw...

...they have round ears and pointed heads.

Mouse from front The body makes two ovals...

...and a long, thin tail with no fur on it.

Rabbit (side view) Rabbits have oval-shaped bodies and heads.

Rabbits can be long- or shorthaired. Which type are you trying to draw?

Rabbit (front view) Rabbits are made up of overlapping circles.

When drawing a rabbit from the front you cannot see its tail.

Ladybug Ladybugs are really easy. Just draw an oval...

...then color it in, adding six legs.

Spiders Spiders are made up of two circles.

Notice where the legs join the body.

Grasshoppers Grasshoppers are flat on top, and curved underneath.

Look carefully at the shape of the legs.

Butterflies Butterflies' wings are like two triangles.

Have fun coloring or painting in the beautiful markings.

 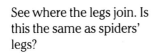 

Beetles Beetles' bodies are made of two ovals.

See where the legs join. Is this the same as spiders' legs?

Patch says... Remember that the same animal's body will be made up of different shapes depending on whether you are seeing it from the front, the side, or from above.

27

Stencils and templates

Stencils and templates are really two versions of the same idea. They are both cut-out shapes you use to make a picture. With a stencil, you use the shape you have cut out *inside* your cardboard or paper; with a template, you draw around the *outside* of the shape. Both stencils and templates can be used again and again, either in the same picture, or to make other pictures.

If you use them carefully, stencils and templates give a very neat outline, so they are ideal for any pets that have a sleek silhouette – such as shorthaired cats or dogs, or goldfish, for example. Remember to keep the shape simple so that it is easier to cut out and work with.

You will need

- thin cardboard or thick paper
- pencil
- eraser
- scissors
- paper (for your picture)
- paints
- stiff brush (or special stencil brush)

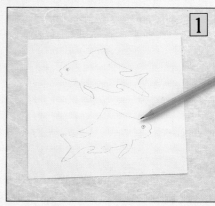

For a stencil, draw your pet on the cardboard, leaving a wide border around the edge.

Carefully cut away the *inside* of the shape you have drawn. If you have drawn an awkward shape, ask for help cutting it out.

Hold your stencil firmly down on the paper, and paint inside.

Lift the stencil off carefully, then add any other details you want (below).

1

For a template, draw your cat as before.

2

Cut out the shape, leaving the edge this time. If you are very careful, you can make a stencil and a template at the same time.

3

Lay your template down on the paper, and draw around the edge.

The tortoise and dog can be used to make stencils. Trace them from the book. Cut away the head, body and leg shapes separately, leaving the connecting bits of card, to create a traditional stencil effect. The parrot can be used for either a stencil or a template.

4

Lift off the template, then fill in the outline with paint.

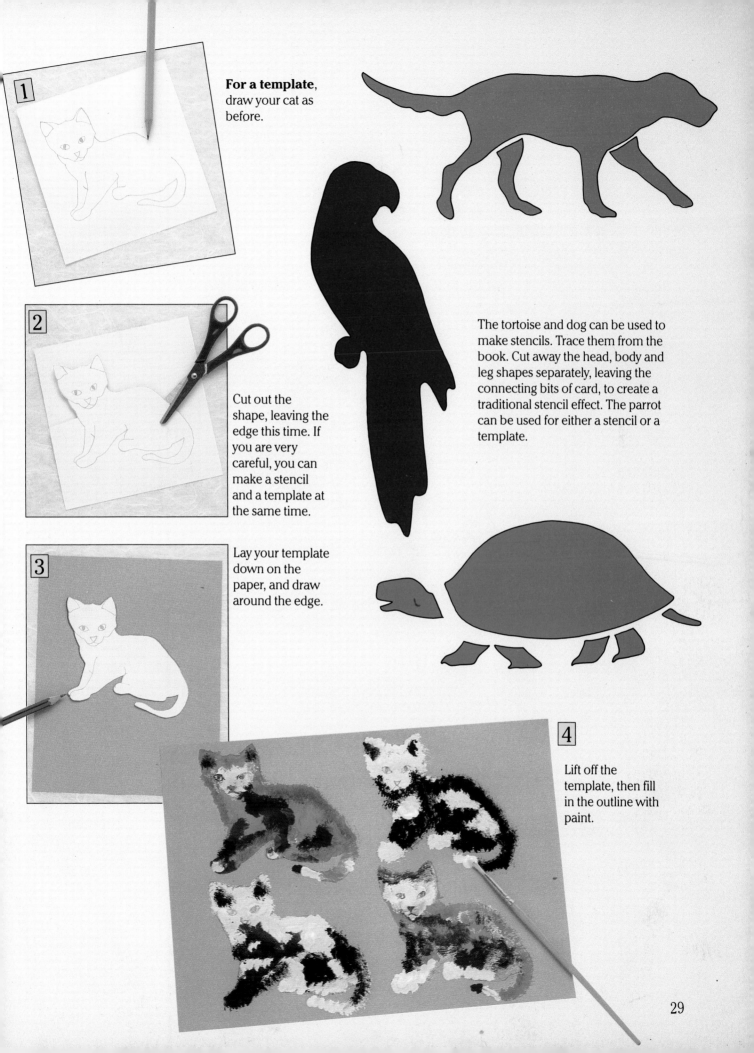

Mixing color

Colors are divided into three groups – *primary, secondary,* and *tertiary* (pronounced "ter-shary"). The *primary colors* are red, yellow, and blue, and they cannot be mixed from other colors. But all other colors, except white, can be made from mixtures of these three.

Secondary colors are made from two primary colors. Green is made from blue and yellow, orange from red and yellow, and violet from red and blue. *Tertiary colors* are made from one primary and one secondary color.

Look carefully at colors you see around you and compare them. There is more than just one blue, for example. Some blues have more red in them and look like purple; others have more yellow and look like green. Practice mixing colors to figure out what you need to add to change one color into another.

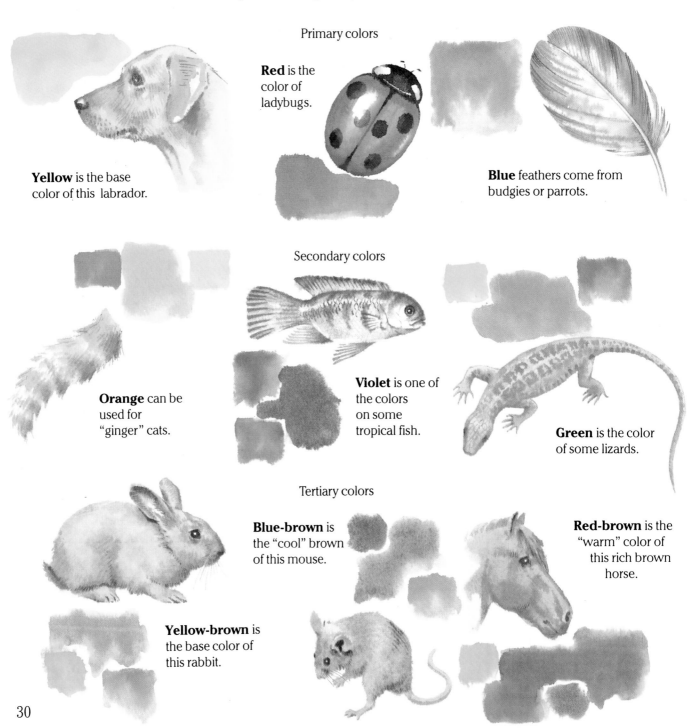

Primary colors

Yellow is the base color of this labrador.

Red is the color of ladybugs.

Blue feathers come from budgies or parrots.

Secondary colors

Orange can be used for "ginger" cats.

Violet is one of the colors on some tropical fish.

Green is the color of some lizards.

Tertiary colors

Blue-brown is the "cool" brown of this mouse.

Red-brown is the "warm" color of this rich brown horse.

Yellow-brown is the base color of this rabbit.

A color wheel

This wheel is divided into three circles. In the middle there are the three primary colors, red, yellow and blue. Next there are the secondary colors made from mixing the two primaries next to them. You can see that yellow and blue make green, red and blue make purple, and red and yellow make orange. The outside circle shows the tertiary colors, made by mixing the secondary colors that are next to each other. If you count up the colors in the wheel, you will see that there are nine in all – starting from just three primaries.

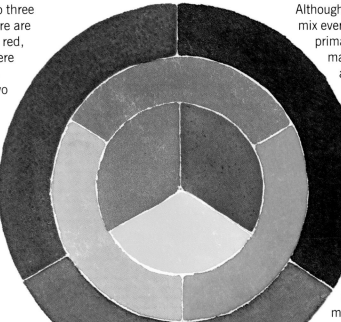

Colors to buy
Although it should be possible to mix every color from just the three primaries, the problem is that many of the reds, yellows, and blues you buy are already mixtures themselves. You will find it easier to have a few ready-mixed secondary and tertiary colors as well.

To start your collection, you should have at least the three primaries and the three secondaries, plus white, black, and perhaps a tan color, such as yellow ocher, and a medium brown. When you find out which colors you use most, you can always buy a few more.

cool violet-gray

warm yellow-brown

Warm and cool colors
Have you ever thought of colors being "warm" or "cool"? Red and orange – the colors of fire – are warm colors, blue and green – the colors of water – are cool colors. Browns and grays can also be warm or cool, depending on how much red or blue they contain.

warm red-brown

cool yellow-gray

Patch says... If you are painting with gouache or poster paint and you want to make a color paler, add a little white. But if you do this with watercolor, it will only make the paint go dull and muddy-looking. To make watercolor paler, just add a little water to thin the paint.

If you want to make a color darker, add some black, but not too much.

31

Mixing browns

"My dog's brown," says a friend. Well, most mammals are brown, so it doesn't tell you much about your friend's dog. You'd want to know if it's dark brown, light brown, a reddish brown, a sandy-colored brown, an orangey tea brown or a chocolate brown. In other words, there are many different browns, and you will need to mix the right one if you want a realistic painting of your pet.

Try mixing some of the browns below and then experiment by adding a little more of one of the colors to the wet paint and see how it changes the resulting color.

This pale, sandy-colored-turtle brown is made from mainly the yellow and the orange, with a little gray and a tiny spot of green. The green and the gray stop the brown from being too reddish.

The pale brown on this cat was made with more yellow than gray paint. The darker brown used more gray than yellow. The artist also used pink on the ears and nose.

The dark brown patches on this dog were made by mixing equal parts of red, yellow, and blue paint. Look at the difference between this and the hamster, which was also done with the same colors in pencil.

This reddish-brown is made of blue and red, which you might think would make a purple horse! In fact, very little blue was used, and the red paint is actually an orange-red, which means it's already fairly close to brown.

This hamster is drawn in red, blue, and yellow colored pencils, using about the same amount of each. Look carefully to see the single pencil strokes.

watercolor paint

crayon

felt-tip pen

colored pencil

chalk

This is a painting of two dogs. Or is it? Look carefully, and you'll find some other animals hidden in the picture. The picture has been done in nothing but browns, and the artist has used a mixture of watercolor paints, colored pencils, colored felt-tips, and chalk pastel crayons. **Watercolor** is good for quickly brushing over large areas of solid color where you want to cover the white paper completely and don't need any detail. You can thin it out to make very pale colors. **Colored pencils** are good for detail but can also be used to cover quite large areas. Depending on how hard you press, you can make a color light or dark. As you can see on the dogs' hair, you can get interesting, uneven mixes of color with pencils. **Felt-tips** are excellent for adding strong-colored detail such as outlines and eyes. **Chalk pastel crayons** are fairly thick and are good for covering large areas. Pastels can give strong colors. Add them last because they smudge.

Special effects with paint

T here are many different ways of using paint other than just painting it on with a brush. Keep experimenting with ways of applying it – not only will your paintings look much more interesting, but you will also enjoy doing them even more.

Here are just a few ideas to get you started.

Adding detail This beetle was painted in two greens. The shine on its back was left unpainted, and black pastel was used for detail.

Applying highlights This goldfish was painted in two oranges. The main highlight was left unpainted, but white paint was added for the highlights on the head and eye.

Pale washes These lovebirds were first painted in very pale washes. The feathers and other details were then built up with colored pencil.

Blending colors A pale, pinky-brown wash was first painted on this cat. A darker brown was then added while the wash was still wet so that the colors blended.

Creating soft effects The spots on this rabbit were added while the paint underneath was still wet. This made them spread and look soft and "splotchy."

Using a thin brush A thin brush was used to paint lines for the hair on this pinky-brown mouse. Notice how the lines follow the shape of the body.

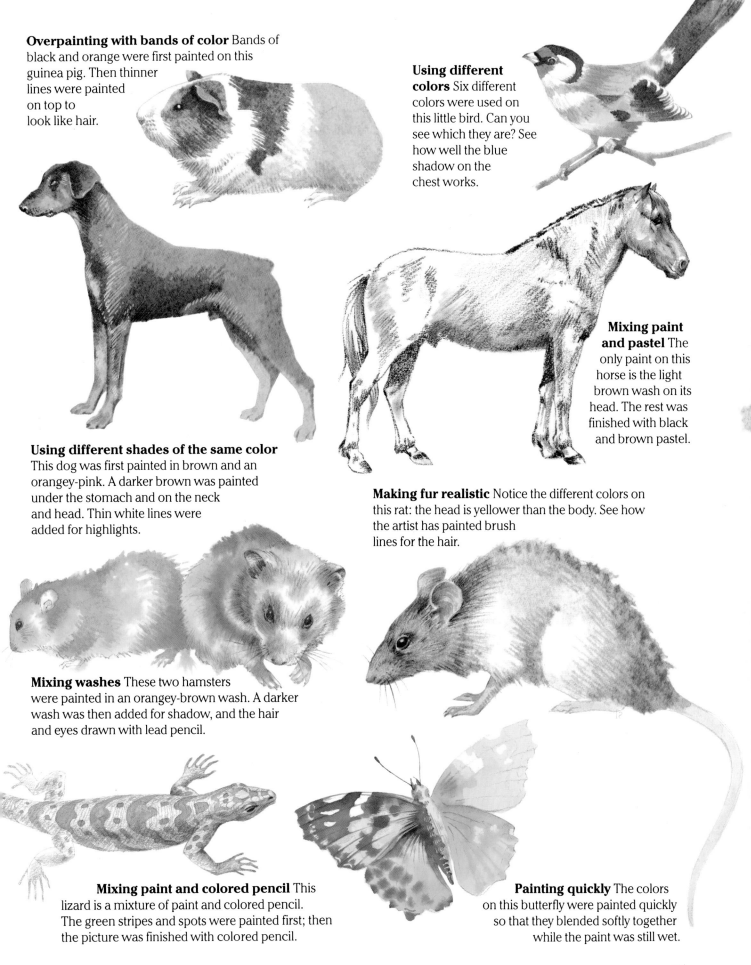

Overpainting with bands of color Bands of black and orange were first painted on this guinea pig. Then thinner lines were painted on top to look like hair.

Using different colors Six different colors were used on this little bird. Can you see which they are? See how well the blue shadow on the chest works.

Mixing paint and pastel The only paint on this horse is the light brown wash on its head. The rest was finished with black and brown pastel.

Using different shades of the same color This dog was first painted in brown and an orangey-pink. A darker brown was painted under the stomach and on the neck and head. Thin white lines were added for highlights.

Making fur realistic Notice the different colors on this rat: the head is yellower than the body. See how the artist has painted brush lines for the hair.

Mixing washes These two hamsters were painted in an orangey-brown wash. A darker wash was then added for shadow, and the hair and eyes drawn with lead pencil.

Mixing paint and colored pencil This lizard is a mixture of paint and colored pencil. The green stripes and spots were painted first; then the picture was finished with colored pencil.

Painting quickly The colors on this butterfly were painted quickly so that they blended softly together while the paint was still wet.

35

Cats

Cats can bend and stretch their bodies into all sorts of interesting shapes, so they are wonderful animals to draw or paint.

Although there aren't as many types of cat as there are dogs, cats do vary in shape. There are roughly three kinds of shape. Some cats are long and thin, with pointed faces, big ears, and long, elegant legs. Others have such long fur that they look like big, round balls of fluff, although underneath all that fur, their bodies are quite skinny. Somewhere in between these two is the shape that most ordinary cats have – a fairly round body with a head and legs that aren't too long. Is this the shape of your cat?

long, curved body

stretched up at back, tail curled forward

wide body, short legs

Look at all these different silhouettes of cats. Notice how the length of a cat's fur affects its shape. Which of these silhouettes looks most like your cat? Choose that one to copy, starting by drawing the inner shapes first (see page 24).

slim body, long legs

arched back, head lowered

triangle-shaped seated cat

36

oval shape, legs folded
under, big ears

wide back, tail
stretched out

short legs, wide body and
tail, small ears

long, lean body,
pointed head

long legs, tail tucked in

narrow body, big ears

square head, wide
body, short legs

high at front sloping
down to tail

big ears, narrow head,
long legs

37

Close-up on cats

How would you start to draw a cat's head? Would you draw a circle for the face and two triangles for the ears? That would probably be fine for most cats, but have you ever compared the shape of different cats' heads? Just as different kinds of cat have different-shaped bodies, so they have different-shaped heads.

Long, thin cats tend to have long, narrow, pointed faces, with big, pointed ears. Very fluffy cats have round, flat faces with what appear to be very small ears because their ears are hidden by their long fur. Most cats' heads are a mixture of these two types. Look at the pictures below to see the difference.

To draw a cat's face, begin as you would for its body: draw the inner shapes first, then draw the outline around them.

Types of head

A fluffy Persian type.
Round, flat face, small ears.

A smooth Siamese.
Narrow, pointed face, big ears.

An ordinary ginger tomcat.
Round face, medium-sized ears.

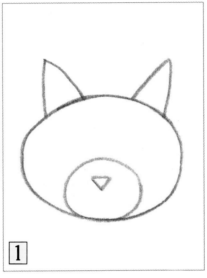

1

Cats' heads are easy. Start with two circles, then add triangles for the ears and a little triangle for the nose.

2

Draw circles for the eyes and below the nostrils, and add a line inside the ears to show the fold in the ear.

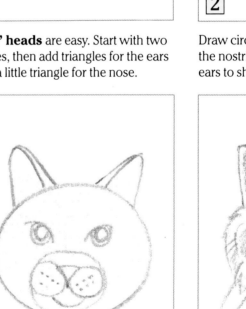

3

Draw another circle for the pupil of the eye (the black part). Make some dots for the whisker ends.

4

Draw the whiskers and sketch in a few hairs around the nose and ears. Shade in the drawing.

Cats' eyes

The pupil in a cat's eye changes depending on how much light there is. If it is bright and sunny, the pupil will be just a narrow slit, like this.

If it is dark, the pupil will be large and round, with just a sliver of the iris (the colored part) showing.

Patch says . . .
Don't forget to add a flash of white for the "glint" in a cat's eye!

Tails

Cats' tails are easy to draw – just start with a line . . .

. . . up in the air

. . . stretched out on the floor

. . . curled around the cat's body

Paws

Cats have five toes on their paws but they are not easy to see because they are covered with fur.

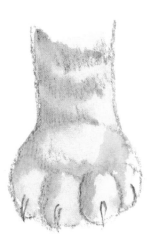

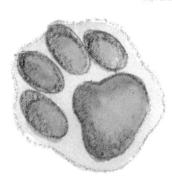

You can see the toes most clearly from underneath.

When the cat's claws are out, ready to scratch, they make a curved shape.

39

Midnight cat

Here is a really dramatic way to do a "night-time" picture of your pet, using just wax crayons and black ink.

When drawing and coloring in with the wax crayons, don't be tempted to use them too much. The finished picture should contain more black areas than color. After all, it is supposed to be nighttime, and the only thing that should really stand out is your pet! In the picture of the "midnight cat" opposite, the less important details such as the houses in the background are shown with just a simple crayon outline. The only details that have been heavily colored in, to make them stand out, are the moon and the cat's eyes. Too much color would have made a much less dramatic picture.

You will need
- a sheet of white paper
- wax crayons
- black writing ink (not waterproof)
- soft paintbrush

A wax crayon cat Draw and color your pet in wax crayons, using different marks for different parts. Lots of short lines could show fur, for example.

Brush ink right over your picture. The ink will not stick to the greasy crayon, so the picture shows through.

40

The finished picture looks completely different once you've added the black ink – it's really quite spooky now! You can see from this picture of the midnight cat that paler colors stand out much more than darker ones. It's worth remembering this when you want to make special effects or to make certain parts of your pet's body stand out more than others.

3

This turtle has been done using watercolor paint instead of ink. The turtle and grass were drawn in, and white wax crayon was used for the clouds. Blue watercolor paint was then brushed over the whole picture. Watercolor paint is best used quite watery on wax drawings, because if it is too thick it will cover the wax crayon.

Dogs

Dogs come in many different sizes, colors, and shapes. When you start a picture of your dog, the first thing you must do is get the overall shape right; adding eyes, ears, nose, and tail can come later.

On pages 24 to 27, you saw how it helps to divide an animal's body into several simple shapes, such as circles and ovals. Look carefully at your dog and you will probably notice some triangles and rectangles as well as round shapes. For example, a long, thin dog with a body that gets narrower toward the back is similar to a triangle, and a wide, stocky body is shaped very much like a rectangle. Does your dog's back slope down toward the back legs, or is it straight? Are the legs long or short, and have you ever noticed how the back legs are shaped differently from the front legs?

Noticing all these small differences is important because these are what give each kind of dog its own special look.

When you think you have got the overall shape right, turn to the next page to see how to draw details like the eyes and ears.

Here are some silhouettes of different dogs. Do you see how the length of a dog's coat can affect its shape? Some small dogs with really long coats look as if they have no legs at all! Copy the silhouette that looks most like your own dog.

long, shaggy coat

curly shapes, arching tail

short hair, pattern of spots

squat shape, big head

triangular shape, plumed tail

lean and graceful

long body, droopy face

long, low
rectangle shape

muscular body, square jaw

pointed tail,
square face

legs almost hidden
by coat

big head, huge ears

very long legs

long,
floppy
ears

straight line
from head
to tail

short legs, fleshy neck

rounded shapes,
pompom tail

droopy face,
long tail

tapering head, stocky body

square head,
pointed tail

43

Close-up on dogs

Dogs come in all shapes and sizes, which makes them more difficult to draw than other animals because you cannot use the same basic shapes for all of them. But fortunately, some of the details, such as eyes and noses, are much the same for all dogs. Dogs' heads do vary, but the main difference is in the shape of the noses. There are basically two nose shapes – long and pointed, like an ice cream cone, or tube-shaped and flat at the end.

Ears also have two shapes – triangular or oval. Which of these drawings looks most like your dog?

Tip for long-haired dogs

Always use the basic shapes as your guide, even if your dog has very long hair.

1

Dog with tube-shaped nose Draw a circle for the head, a tube for the nose and an oval for the ear.

2

Put on the basic color and make the ear a little less symmetrical.

3

Add the details, such as nose and eyes, and do a little more shading if necessary.

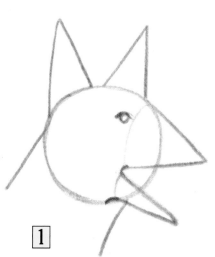

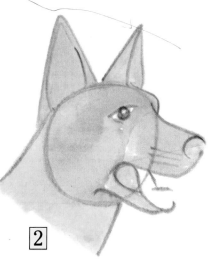

1

Dog with cone-shaped nose Draw a circle for the head and triangles for ears, nose, and jaw.

2

Now draw the curve from the tip of the nose into the mouth. Draw the tongue.

3

Color in the head. The little white speck (highlight) in the eye makes the dog look alert.

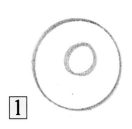

1

Eyes Dogs' eyes are easy. Just start with a circle and then put in another one if you want to have a highlight.

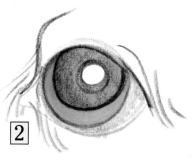

2

Color in a half-moon shape for the brown part of the eye. Use a dark color for the pupil (the black center part) and leave a white highlight.

fifth toe at side

paw print

Paws Here are some pictures of dogs' paws from different angles. Practice copying them.

1

Noses Because the nostrils are fairly complicated shapes, noses look harder than they are. As long as you start with a triangle you will find it quite easy.

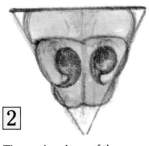

2

The curly edges of the nostrils fit neatly into the triangle. The dark insides make two shapes like commas – or polliwogs.

four toes

toes hidden by long hair

Tails Which of these tails looks most like your dog's?

medium length

plumed

curly

short and stumpy

tufty

long and thin

Spotty dog

Brushes are not the only tools you can use to apply paint – almost anything will do as long as it can make a paint mark on the paper. You could use your fingers, knives (not sharp ones!), forks, or combs, for example, or you could spread the paint across your picture with a piece of cardboard. Each of these tools will make a different kind of mark, and you should remember this when choosing which ones to use.

Dabbing paint on with your finger will give you blobs of color, which could be good for the spots on a dog's coat, like those on the dog in the picture opposite. Applying the paint with a cotton ball will give softer, bigger patches of color like the markings on a guinea pig.

Before you start your final picture, experiment with paint and various tools first, to see what kinds of marks you can make. What do the different marks remind you of?

Spotty finger dog Lightly draw the outline of your dog on the paper, changing any parts you don't like until the drawing is the way you want it.

2

Now fill in the outline with paint, using a finger, fork, comb, or whatever tool you choose. Remember to wash your finger if you change colors!

You will need
- thick paint (such as poster paint)
- tools to apply paint
- paper
- pencil
- eraser

3

Your pet's portrait is finished. Doesn't he look proud and spotty!

Using a sponge This puppy was done with a sponge. The fluffy effect was done by dabbing the sponge very lightly.

Using a flexible knife This cheerful spotted dog was done with paint on the end of a bendy knife. The spots were added with fingertips.

Using cotton swabs This thoughtful dog was done with cotton swabs (often used for eye makeup). Because they are so small, you can dab paint exactly where you want it.

47

Hamsters, rabbits, and gerbils

D o you have a rabbit or a hamster, or some other similar pet? If you do, you have probably noticed how your pet looks like a small, round cushion when it is sitting down, with its legs and feet tucked up neatly by its side. But have you seen how much its shape changes when it is doing other things? When a rabbit is sitting up on its hind legs, for example, it becomes longer and flatter. Hamsters and mice can make themselves much longer and thinner so that they can squeeze through small spaces.

Practice drawing the different shapes these animals make, with details like eyes, nose, and feet.

Feet

Draw the basic shapes of the foot, then add the toes. Always check that you are drawing the right number of toes.

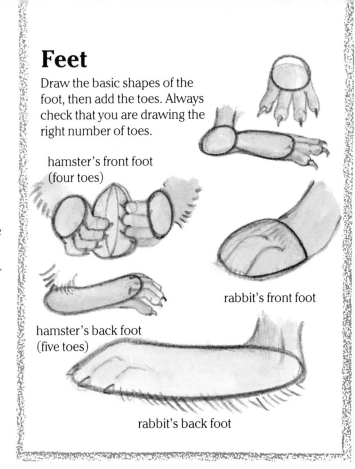

hamster's front foot (four toes)

rabbit's front foot

hamster's back foot (five toes)

rabbit's back foot

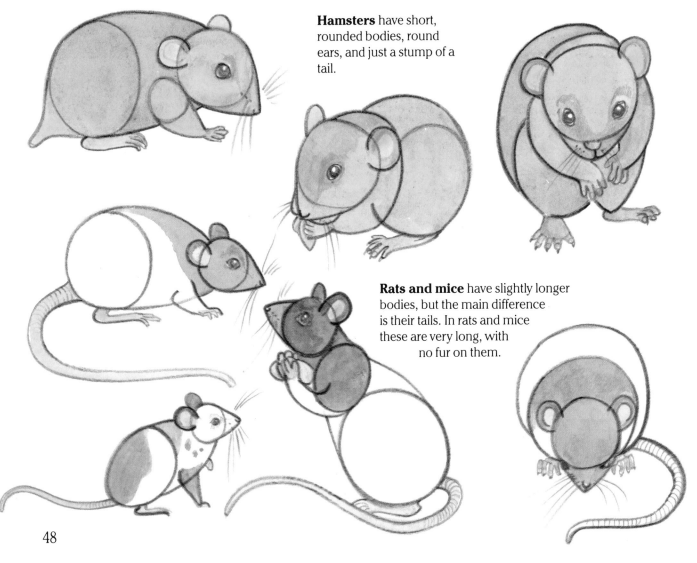

Hamsters have short, rounded bodies, round ears, and just a stump of a tail.

Rats and mice have slightly longer bodies, but the main difference is their tails. In rats and mice these are very long, with no fur on them.

Rabbits have long bodies, which you can see best when they are moving or sitting up. Their ears are long too, and when seen from the side, their heads make an oval shape.

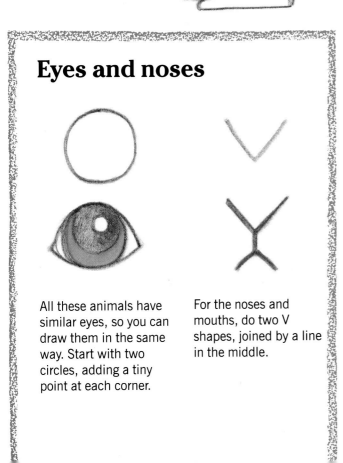

Eyes and noses

All these animals have similar eyes, so you can draw them in the same way. Start with two circles, adding a tiny point at each corner.

For the noses and mouths, do two V shapes, joined by a line in the middle.

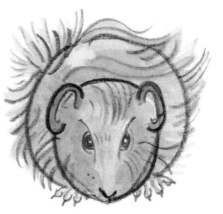

Guinea pigs have short bodies and very large heads. They come in a variety of colors, and some have long hair.

49

Monoprints

Monoprints are exciting because you never know exactly how your finished picture will turn out! A monoprint is like a "backwards" painting. In a painting, you add paint to the paper to make a picture. In a monoprint, you scrape paint away, and instead of working directly on paper, you first make a picture on a metal tray.

You can think of the paint you scrape away on a monoprint in the same way as lines you would add with a brush to an ordinary painting. The green print here was made in this way by scraping an outline in paint on the back of a kitchen tray. But you can get interesting effects if you use scraped lines as highlights, and the paint that's left as shadows.

Try different scrapers for interesting effects. An old toothbrush (not the one you use to clean your teeth!) can make feathery marks and a toothpick or used matchstick is good for details. Use a piece of cardboard to scrape large areas. Try different paper colors also.

Before you do your final print, try some small prints on the corner of the tray until you get the paint thickness right – too much paint will make blobs and spoil your picture.

You will need

- an old metal tea tray or flat baking sheet
- PVA paint mixed with a few drops of dishwashing detergent to slow drying
- a large paintbrush
- paper
- cloth
- different scrapers (such as toothpicks, *used* matchsticks, or pieces of cardboard)

1

A monoprint. Make sure the back of your tray is clean (wash and dry it if it isn't), then paint all over it – the paint washes off easily after printing.

2

Scrape the outlines of your picture using different scrapers for different parts to give your monoprint lots of interesting textures.

50

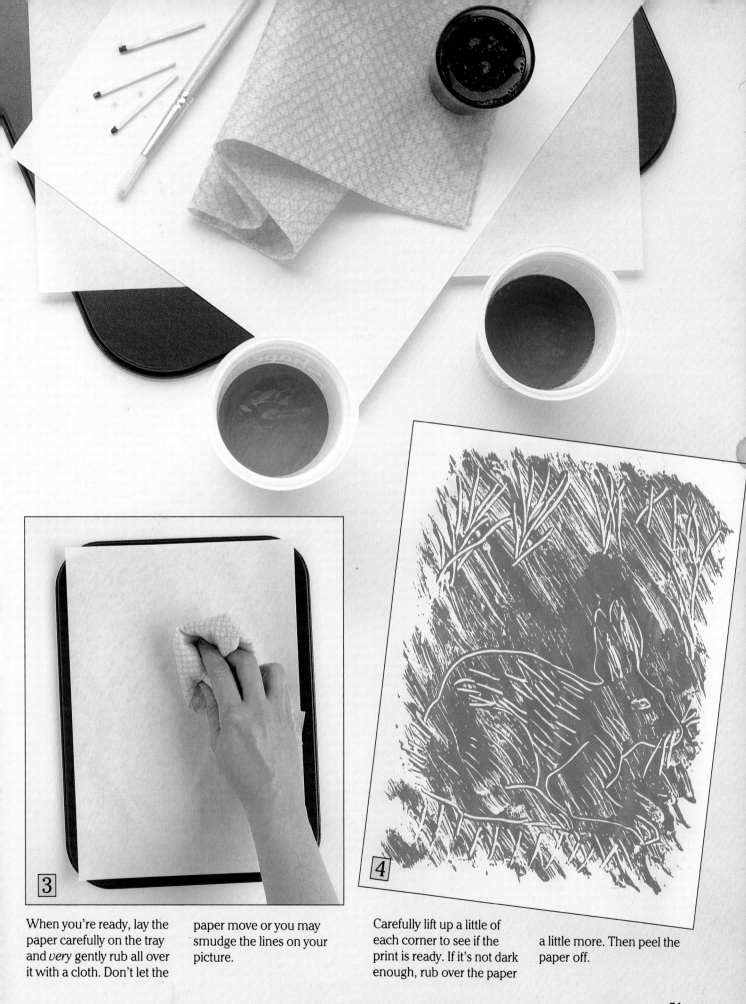

3

When you're ready, lay the paper carefully on the tray and *very* gently rub all over it with a cloth. Don't let the paper move or you may smudge the lines on your picture.

4

Carefully lift up a little of each corner to see if the print is ready. If it's not dark enough, rub over the paper a little more. Then peel the paper off.

Birds

Birds cannot bend and stretch and change their shape in the way cats do, and there are only a few kinds of pet bird – unlike dogs that come in so many different varieties. But this does not mean that they aren't worth drawing or painting – what makes birds really interesting is their beautiful colors.

Because birds have fairly simple shapes, they are one of the easiest pets to draw. All you need to do is a circle for the head, an oval for the body, and a long, pointed tail. You can use these same basic shapes whether you are looking at your bird from the front or from the side.

The only time you can see a bird's wings properly is when it is flying. At other times, it keeps them neatly folded back by its sides.

The most popular pet birds are budgerigars, but some people have larger birds such as parakeets or cockatoos.

Bird shapes Budgerigars can be yellow, green, blue, or gray, or a mixture of these colors. Canaries are smaller, and a lovely yellow all over. Parrots are similar in shape to budgies, but they are much bigger and their colors are brighter. Cockatoos have a wonderful crest of feathers on top of their heads. Finches are smaller than any of the others, and the zebra finch has a jaunty patch of red on its face.

52

Legs and Feet

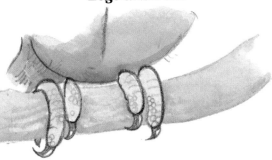

When a bird sits on its perch, it tucks its legs under its body, and curls its claws around the perch to hold on.

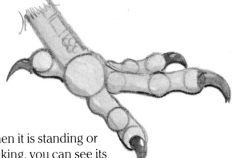

When it is standing or walking, you can see its legs, and its claws are stretched out flat.

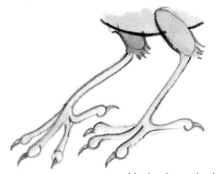

Notice how the legs join on to either side of the body.

Beaks and Eyes

The beaks of budgies, parakeets, and cockatoos are shaped like short triangles. Notice how the top is rounded, and how the end curls over.

Birds' eyes are dark and round, and placed on either side of the head.

The beaks of other pet birds such as canaries or finches come to a straight point at the end.

Feathers

The feathers on the chest and head are short. The feathers on the wings and tail are longer.

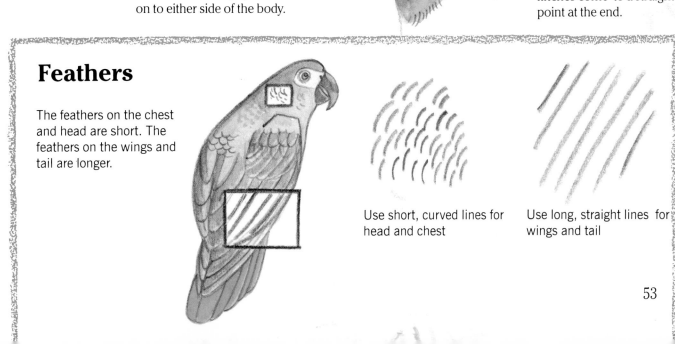

Use short, curved lines for head and chest

Use long, straight lines for wings and tail

53

Paper collage

A collage is a picture made up of pieces of paper, fabric, or other small objects – such as string, beads, dried peas, or corn – all glued onto background paper or cardboard.

If you are making a paper collage, you can use any paper you like: plain-colored paper, patterned wrapping paper, wallpaper, shiny silver or gold candy wrappers, white or colored tissue paper, newspaper, corrugated cardboard, or things made from paper, like straws.

It doesn't matter if the pieces of paper are small, or old and crumpled: just smooth them out and you can still use them. Why not save any pieces of paper you particularly like and build up a collection of scraps especially for your collages?

The paper can be cut into shapes, or you can tear it. Move the pieces around on the background sheet until they look just right, changing any pieces you don't like before you finally stick them down. You can paste the pieces alongside each other, like fitting a jigsaw puzzle together, or you can overlap them.

Lindsey made this parrot collage from paper she colored with crayons. She cut the paper into thin strips and curved each piece by rolling it tightly round a pencil. Finally, she carefully arranged and glued the curved strips in the shape of a parrot.

You will need
- background paper or cardboard
- scraps to paste
- glue
- scissors
- pencil
- eraser

1

Paper parrot Draw your pet's outline on background paper. Cut or tear paper into shapes for different parts. For example, circles and strips make this wing.

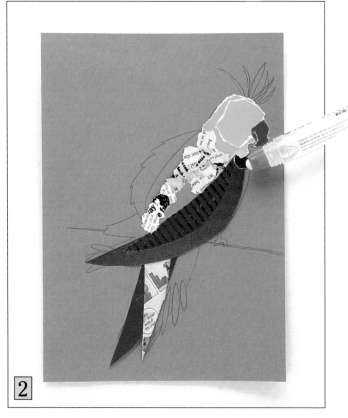

2

Glue down the pieces. To overlap shapes, do the bottom layers first. For example, the long feathers here were stuck first and the small ones added later.

3

As well as using different paper colors and textures, try using transparent colored paper – its color will mix with what shows below to make new colors.

4

A few leaves will finish your collage and give it a jungle feel. Mount backing paper on cardboard.

Fish

I t's fascinating to watch fish swimming about in the underwater world of their tank, darting backward and forward, their tails gently waving in the water.

Fish, like birds, have quite simple shapes that make them easy to draw. All you need to do is one shape for the body, and then add the fins and the tail, and other details like the eyes and mouth.

Goldfish are the commonest pet fish – of course, they aren't really golden, they are a kind of orange color. There are other kinds of pet fish, too, such as tropical fish. Some of these have very beautiful colors and may be striped or spotted. Look carefully to get the colors right. At first glance, you may think that your fish is all one color, but if you look more closely, you may notice delicate changes – some parts may be lighter or darker, or perhaps a little more yellow or silver.

Tips for showing scales

Fish are covered with little scales. Can you think how to show these? Perhaps you could do lots of little curved lines, or zigzag lines going across the body. Stop when you get to the head – the head should look quite smooth. For fin and tail bones, you could do straight lines, fanning out toward the edge.

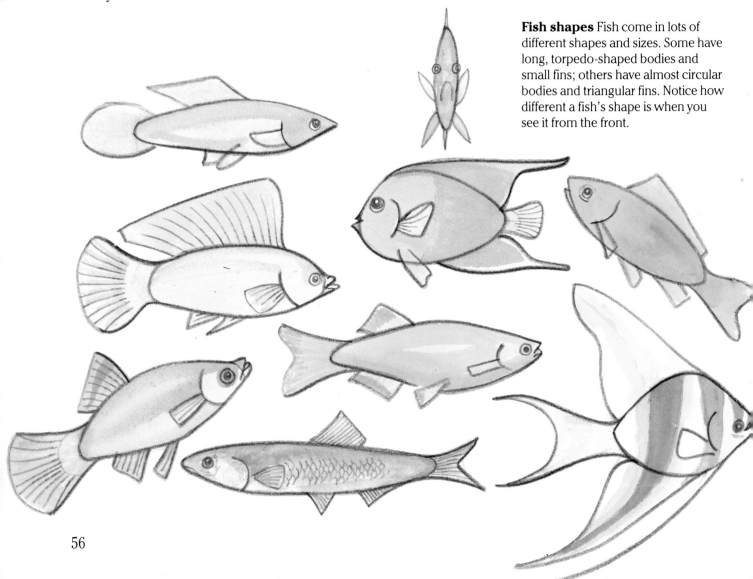

Fish shapes Fish come in lots of different shapes and sizes. Some have long, torpedo-shaped bodies and small fins; others have almost circular bodies and triangular fins. Notice how different a fish's shape is when you see it from the front.

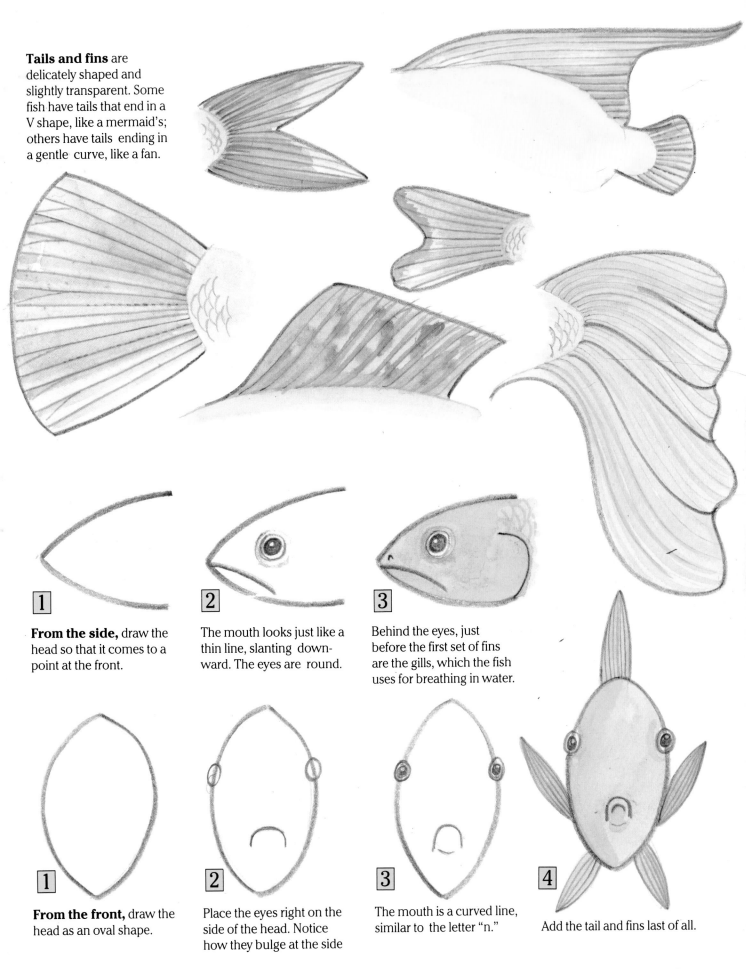

Tails and fins are delicately shaped and slightly transparent. Some fish have tails that end in a V shape, like a mermaid's; others have tails ending in a gentle curve, like a fan.

1 **From the side,** draw the head so that it comes to a point at the front.

2 The mouth looks just like a thin line, slanting downward. The eyes are round.

3 Behind the eyes, just before the first set of fins are the gills, which the fish uses for breathing in water.

1 **From the front,** draw the head as an oval shape.

2 Place the eyes right on the side of the head. Notice how they bulge at the side

3 The mouth is a curved line, similar to the letter "n."

4 Add the tail and fins last of all.

57

Wash-off pictures

W ash-off pictures are fun because you don't know exactly how a finished picture will look. To do one, paint your shapes on cardboard, using paint you mix with water. When the paint is dry, cover the cardboard with waterproof ink. When the ink's dry, wash away the painted shapes, leaving pale silhouettes (the paint stains the cardboard so some color stays). The waterproof ink does not wash off.

You can do just one animal, but wash-off pictures look best if you do lots of the same kind of pet, such as dogs or a tankful of fish, for example.

When you choose colors, think how they will look next to each other in the finished picture.

You will need
- a piece of cardboard
- pencil
- eraser
- thick water-based paint (poster color is ideal)
- waterproof ink
- paintbrush

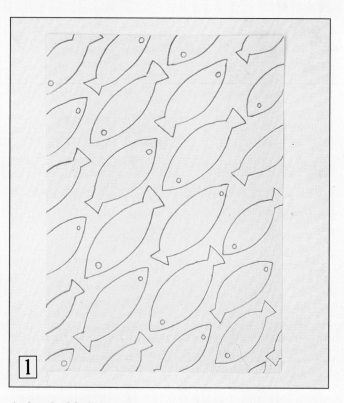

A shoal of fish Draw your animal shapes on the cardboard, rubbing out to correct if necessary. It's best to keep the shapes very simple, so don't add lots of detail. Repeated shapes will look very effective.

Fill in the shapes with the thick paint. You could leave "holes" for the eyes or other details, such as the spots on a spotty dog – the ink you use next will fill in the holes. Let the paint dry completely.

58

3

When you're sure the paint is dry, brush all over the cardboard with waterproof ink – if you do this before the paint is dry, the ink will mix with the paint and blur the shapes and colors and spoil the picture.

5

As you wash off the ink, support the cardboard with both hands so that there is no danger of tearing it. As if by magic, ghostly silhouettes of the fish will start to appear.

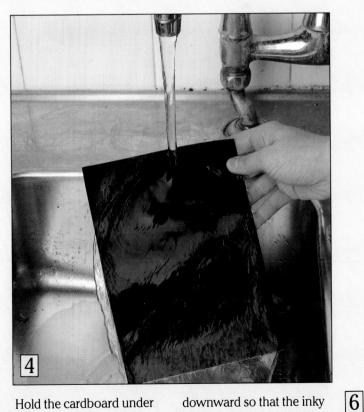

4

Hold the cardboard under some warm water and gently wash off the ink. Hold the cardboard downward so that the inky water runs down into the sink and not all over you!

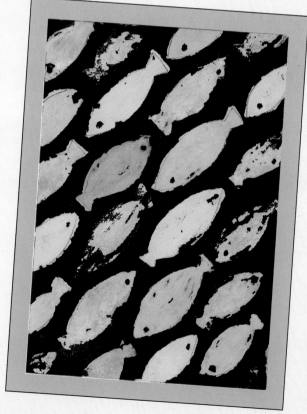

6

Don't your finished fish stand out well against the dark ink! Why not try some different ink colors?

Reptiles

Snakes are more unusual pets than cats, dogs, or rabbits, and they are not everyone's choice. They are certainly wonderful to draw and paint, since they have lovely colors and markings. They also stay still for quite long periods so that you can study them, and when they move, they make marvelous curling shapes.

Quite a lot of people keep lizards as pets, and they are fascinating to watch, darting about, and flicking their tongues in and out. They never stop moving for long, though, so if you want to draw and paint them you will have to observe them carefully.

The best of all "artist's models" are turtles, because they move so slowly that you have plenty of time to copy them! Turtles' bodies are mostly hidden away under their shells so that all you can see are their heads and legs. The shells are shaped like hemispheres – similar to an open umbrella – curling upward slightly at the edges where the head and legs come out.

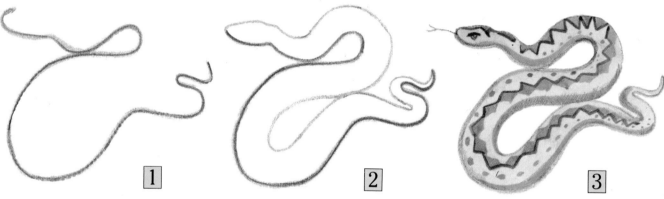

1

2

3

Snakes are the easiest of all pets to draw. Start with a simple line to show the shape.

Notice whether your snake's body is wider than its head. Some snakes have quite thick bodies.

Now color in the markings. You'll enjoy this, particularly if your snake is a colorful one.

Painting scales

Begin by sketching in the pattern in pencil. Notice how the scales overlap one another.

Put on a flat color all over the snake's body.

Now color in the scales in paint or crayon.

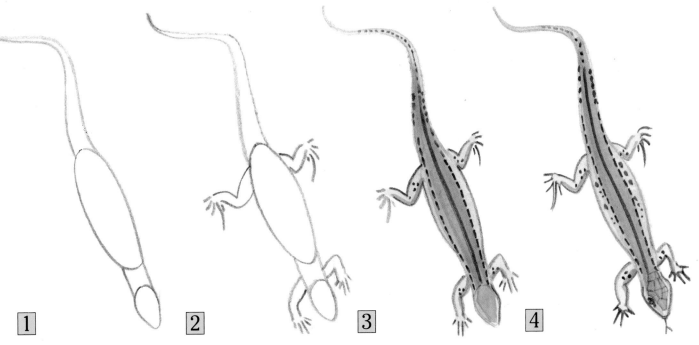

1

Lizards are a little like snakes with legs, but their bodies are wider in the middle.

2

Start with the simple shapes for the body and tail, and then draw the legs.

3

There are different kinds of lizards, so look carefully at yours to see the patterns on its body.

4

You can draw the spots with small straight lines or little blobs.

Different views Here is a turtle seen from the front and the side. Notice how little the basic shape changes, wherever you are looking from.

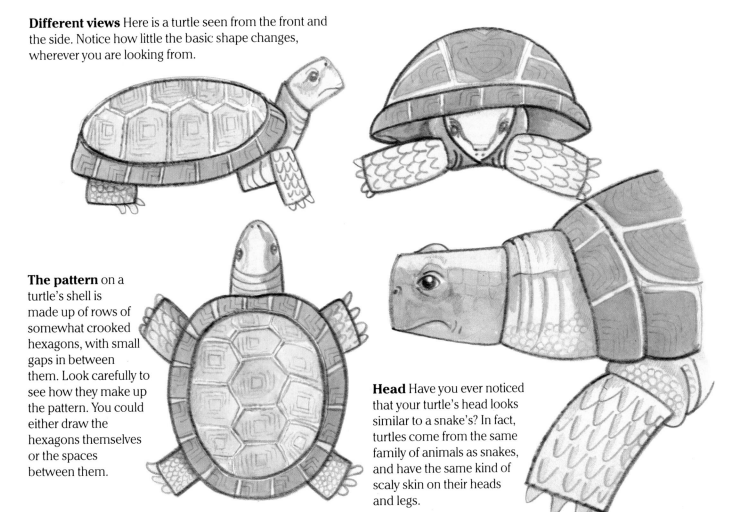

The pattern on a turtle's shell is made up of rows of somewhat crooked hexagons, with small gaps in between them. Look carefully to see how they make up the pattern. You could either draw the hexagons themselves or the spaces between them.

Head Have you ever noticed that your turtle's head looks similar to a snake's? In fact, turtles come from the same family of animals as snakes, and have the same kind of scaly skin on their heads and legs.

Stained-glass windows

H ave you ever been inside a church on a sunny day? If you have, you probably saw some beautiful colored lights on the walls made by sunlight shining in through the stained-glass windows. You can easily make your own stained-glass picture of a favorite animal.

You'll need some thick paper or thin cardboard that light will not show through, and some see-through colored tissue or candy wrappers. It's best to use dark-colored cardboard or paper so that the tissue shows up well. Cutting holes in the cardboard or paper and sticking tissue over them will let light shine through to make your picture. If you are very careful, you can use a craft knife to cut out the holes. Besides being careful not to cut your own fingers, don't leave a sharp knife lying around where someone else might cut themselves on it! Or you can use scissors instead.

You will need
- colored tissue paper or clear colored candy wrappers
- thick colored paper or cardboard
- scissors or a craft knife
- pencil
- eraser
- glue
- tape

1

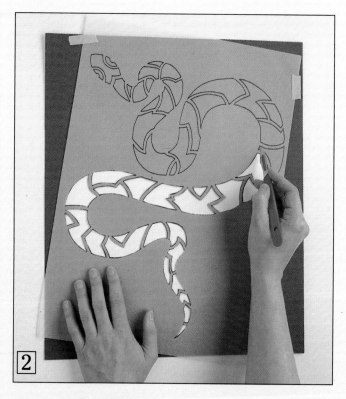

2

Using a craft knife to make a stained-glass snake Draw a snake in simple, strong lines on tracing paper. Add shapes for cut-out holes for the tissue paper. Leave wide enough strips between each hole onto which to glue the tissue.

Tape the tracing paper on a piece of cardboard so it won't slip when you cut the holes. Lay the cardboard on something that doesn't matter if it gets cut – don't use the dining table! Cut out the shapes with a craft knife – *it's very sharp, so take care!*

Patch says ...
you can color plain tracing paper with felt-tip pens, crayons, or pencils instead of using tissue paper, as in the turtle and snail here.

When you have cut the holes, lay colored tissue under the cardboard and trace around the holes onto the tissue. Cut the tissue with scissors, leaving a little extra all round the pencil line for gluing. Spread a little glue round the hole and fix on the tissue.

When you finish your stained-glass picture, tape it to a window that gets lots of strong sunlight. If you like, add a nice frame to your snake, just like a real church window. (Use a ruler to draw and cut straight lines.)

Insects

Stick insects have a very clever disguise to fool other creatures that might want to eat them – they look exactly like sticks or twigs, and this is how they got their name. To make the disguise even better, they are a beautiful green color, just like the stems and leaves they live on – sometimes it's almost impossible to see them.

Other insects you might keep as "pets" for a short time are ladybugs and ants. Perhaps you have an ant or ladybug colony in a shoebox, full of soil and leaves and twigs. Although it is fascinating to watch these little creatures, it's best not to keep ants and ladybugs indoors for too long before you put them back outside.

Stick insects, ladybugs, and ants all have three pairs of legs, but their body shapes are quite different.

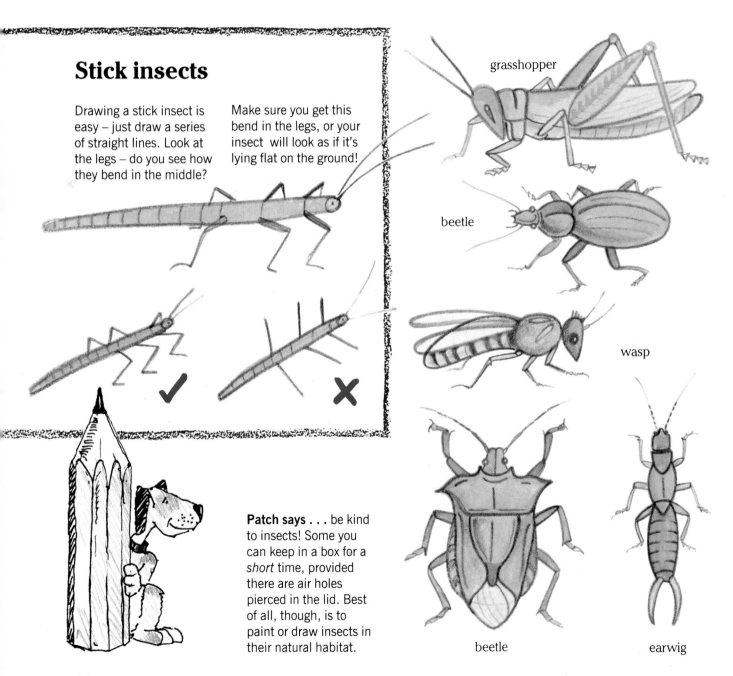

Stick insects

Drawing a stick insect is easy – just draw a series of straight lines. Look at the legs – do you see how they bend in the middle?

Make sure you get this bend in the legs, or your insect will look as if it's lying flat on the ground!

grasshopper

beetle

wasp

Patch says . . . be kind to insects! Some you can keep in a box for a *short* time, provided there are air holes pierced in the lid. Best of all, though, is to paint or draw insects in their natural habitat.

beetle

earwig

64

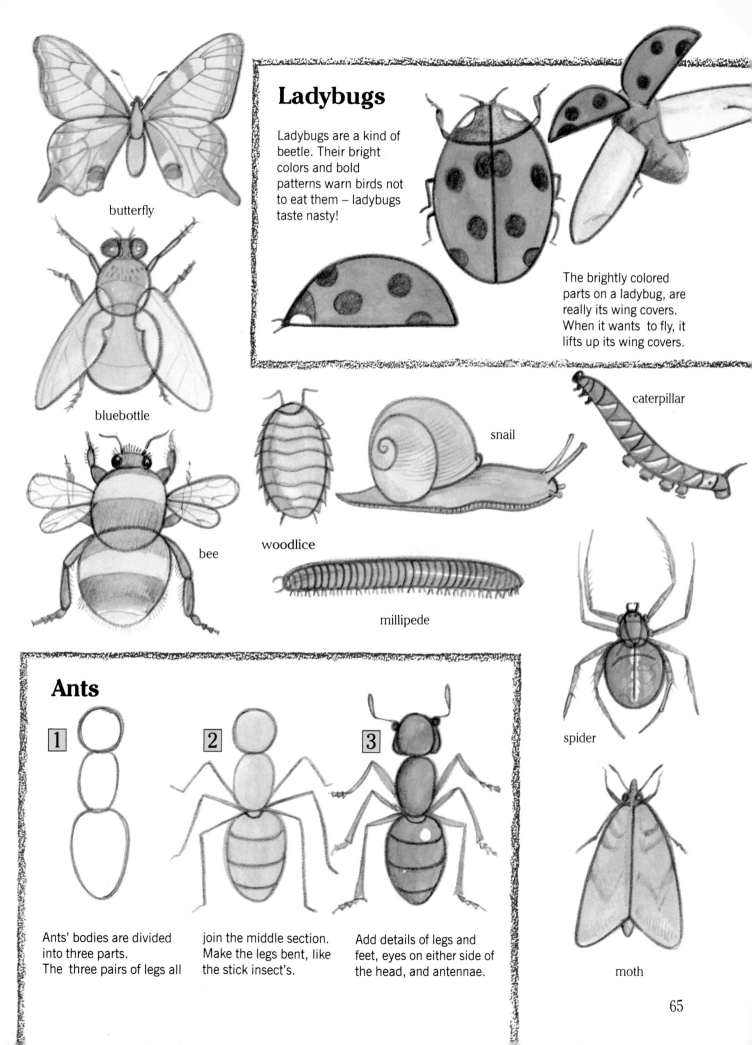

butterfly

Ladybugs

Ladybugs are a kind of beetle. Their bright colors and bold patterns warn birds not to eat them – ladybugs taste nasty!

The brightly colored parts on a ladybug, are really its wing covers. When it wants to fly, it lifts up its wing covers.

bluebottle

caterpillar

snail

bee

woodlice

millipede

spider

Ants

1

2

3

Ants' bodies are divided into three parts. The three pairs of legs all

join the middle section. Make the legs bent, like the stick insect's.

Add details of legs and feet, eyes on either side of the head, and antennae.

moth

Scratch pictures

Have you ever done a scratchboard picture, where you scratch through the top layer to show the color below? You can buy scratchboards in stores, but it's much cheaper and more fun to make your own. Most bought scratchboards are white underneath, so you get white drawings on black backgrounds (there are a few other colors, too, such as bronze or silver). One of the best things about making your own scratchboards is that you can have any color you want and as many of them as you like.

It's best to use light, bright colors on the base, otherwise they won't contrast enough with the black

and your drawing won't show up very well. You can use colors similar to your pet's, such as orange, yellow, or brown, or you can make a "rainbow" effect with, say, green, red, and blue, which would be good for brightly colored tropical fish or birds.

When you paint black over the colors, it's hard to know where colors begin and end, but you'll have a rough idea. For example, if you want your dog sitting on the grass, you can color the bottom of the board green, so when you scratch that area, green will show through.

You can use all sorts of things for scratching. Pins, nails, forks, coins, or your fingernails are just a few ideas. A mixture of different lines – thick or thin, straight or wavy – will add interest to your picture, so use different tools to draw different parts of your pet. A fork, for example, could make wavy lines that look like fur.

You will need
- piece of white cardboard
- wax crayons
- black paint
- dishwashing detergent
- paintbrush
- scratching tools

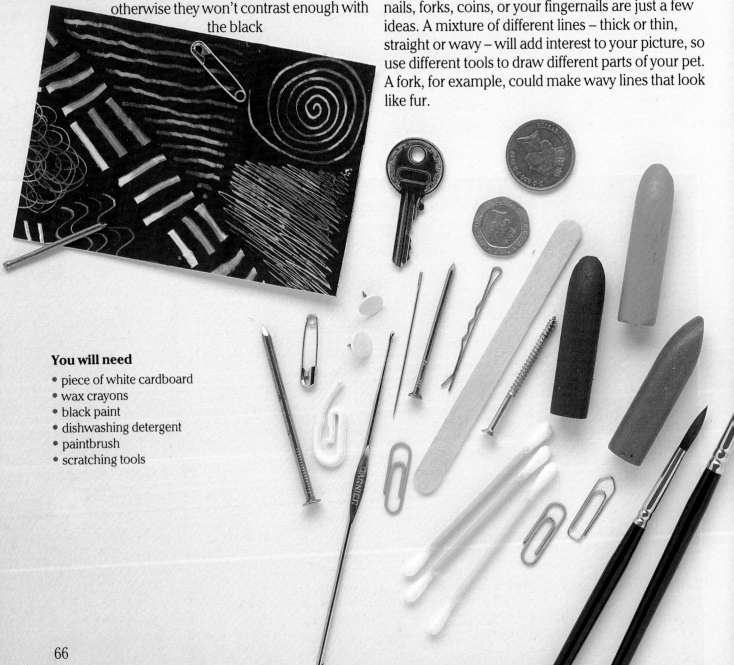

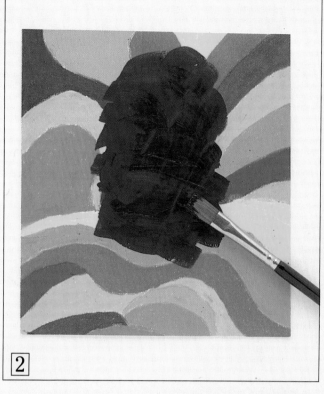

1

2

Rainbow scratch bugs and butterflies color the cardboard with the crayons, thinking about where you want each color to be in your finished picture.

Mix the paint with a few drops of dishwashing detergent. This will give it the right thickness, which should be like thick cream. Brush over the cardboard.

3

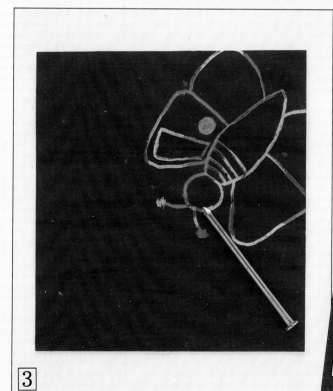

4

Wait until the paint is completely dry before you start using your scratchboard. Scratch out a picture and watch the colors appear.

The colors underneath are revealed, producing multi-colored insects.

Horses and ponies

People who enjoy riding often like horse pictures to remind them of their "four-legged friends." Horses and ponies can be quite difficult to draw because they have a more complicated shape than many other animals, but if you begin by copying the ones on these two pages, you should be able to get quite a good likeness.

Notice how many shapes go to make up the silhouette of a pony. Compare the front and back legs – they really look quite different. The front legs are straight and more or less the same width all the way up; the back legs are very wide at the top and almost come to a point in the middle.

Drawing from the side

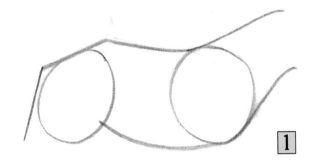

1

Ponies' bodies are mostly made up of circles and ovals.

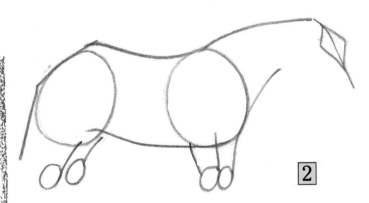

2

Draw the circles for the body and then the smaller ones for the knees.

Pony and rider

Why not do a picture of yourself on your pony? Draw the pony first, then use the "stick person" guide here to help you draw yourself. Finally, fill in the colors.

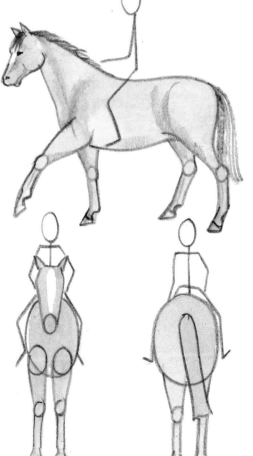

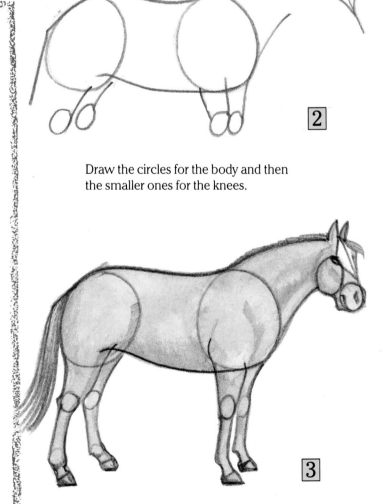

3

When you have finished the outline, color in the body and put in some shading to make it look nice and round.

Drawing from the front

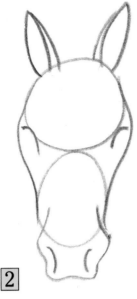

1
Start with two circles and pointed ovals for the ears. Then draw the shape for the nose.

2
Draw curves for the top eyelid, and the same curves the other way around for the nostrils.

3
Draw lines down to the nose for the sharp bone that gives the face its shape. Finish off by shading in the eyes and forelock.

Types of horse and pony Look at the difference in size and proportion between different types of horses and ponies.

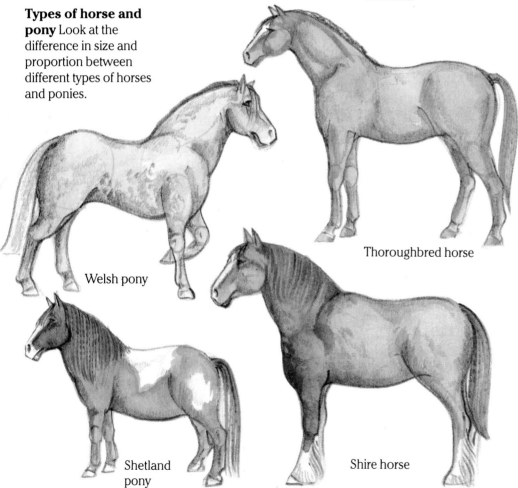

Welsh pony

Shetland pony

Thoroughbred horse

Shire horse

pony with correct proportions.

pony with legs too short.

pony with legs too long.

pony with head too big.

Getting the proportions right
Try to get the "proportions" of your pony right. This means getting the parts the right size for each other. If you make the legs too short, the body will look too heavy and fat; if you make them too long, your pony will look too skinny!

Close-up on horses

 hen you have got the general shape of your pony or horse right, you can begin to fill in the details. These drawings show you how to do them.

1 **Horses' heads** are made up of circles joined by straight lines. Start with these.

2 Put in the eye near the top of the big circle. It fits just under the brow bone, which makes a triangle shape.

3 Put in the nostrils, mouth, and forelock, and shade in the drawing.

Ears Horses' and ponies' ears are shaped like triangles.

Eyes They have soft, gentle eyes, placed on either side of the head. Notice how the eyelids bulge out above the eyes.

Nostrils Their nostrils are large, and slant down toward the front of the nose.

Donkeys

Donkeys have much longer ears than horses and ponies, and their manes and forelocks stand up like brushes.

70

Techniques for heads and manes

Heads
Start with a drawing in light pencil, and then use paint or crayons to fill in the ponies' main color. If your pony has a white blaze like this one, go around the edges carefully. Color in the forelock, mane, and eyes last.

Manes
Horse's manes flop down between their ears, and down the sides of the neck. You can draw them with wavy lines or paint them with a thin brush. Manes and tails are usually darker than their coats.

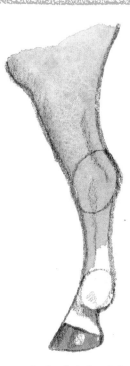

Legs and hoofs
Horses' legs are a lovely knobby shape. Notice how the front leg goes in and out above and below the knee.

Hoofs Horses wear "shoes" to protect their hoofs. They are made to fit around the underneath of the hoof.

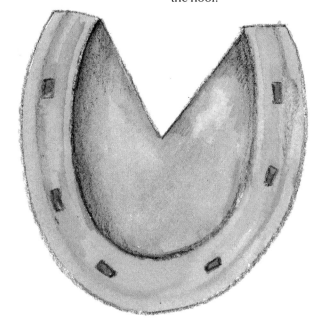

The back leg is much thicker at the top than the front one. When you're drawing horses' and ponies' legs don't forget to put in the little knob just above the hoof, at the back of the leg – it is one of the most distinctive features of a horse's leg.

Allsorts collage

You can make a collage from almost anything as long as you can paste it down on cardboard or paper. If you like doing collage, it's a good idea to build up a collection of materials you could use, such as scraps of paper, fabric, wool or string, buttons, paper clips, seeds, pieces of pasta, toothpicks, and so on.

When it comes to making your collage, choose suitable items from your collection according to the color, pattern, or texture of the subject they are representing.

You will need
- thick paper or cardboard
- all-purpose glue
- pencil or ballpoint pen
- eraser
- light and dark brown felt
- pieces of wool
- string
- toothpicks
- colored tissue paper
- foil paper
- green fabric
- poppy seeds
- pearl barley

Cut out the main shapes for your collage. If necessary, draw them first with a pencil, or a pen if you are drawing on fabric. Cut out the shapes just inside the outline so that it won't show.

Arrange the shapes on the cardboard the way you like them, then glue them in place. Finally add the smaller details like eyes or ears.

Patch says... Think about what you are trying to show, and use the item that looks most like it. For example, what could you use for whiskers – toothpicks, silver paper, string, or nylon line? Dried peas, buttons, or seeds could be good for eyes, and so on. The picture shows a few of the items you can add to your collection.

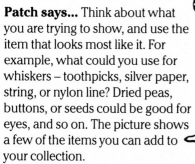

Different colored patches of felt and paper were used for the rabbit's coat, and rough, woolly fabric was used to create the effect of the cat's fur. Pieces of fabric in different colors and patterns were used to create the rainbow fish.

Cartoons

Cartoon animals are not meant to look like real-life animals, but they can do all sorts of things that real animals cannot do, such as smiling, frowning, walking about on two legs, and so on.

Some of the most famous cartoon characters are animals. How many can you think of? There are Mickey and Minnie Mouse, Donald Duck, Bugs Bunny, Tom and Jerry, Snoopy, and the Teenage Mutant Turtles. Can you think of any others?

Cartoon animals have exaggerated shapes – they may have extra big heads, noses, or feet, for example. The other difference from real-life animals is that cartoon animals look a lot more "human" and can have the same expressions on their faces as people. So, if you want to do a picture showing how your pet is feeling, why not do a cartoon?

Have a look at your pet. What is it doing at this moment? Perhaps it is going to sleep, or playing. Try to imagine what its feelings are – do you think it feels sad, or happy, or tired? Here are some hints to help you to get the right expression on your pet's face.

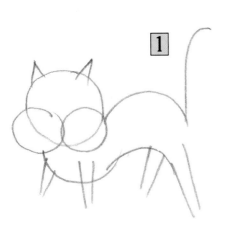

How to draw a cartoon pet Start drawing your cartoon animal in the same way as other animals, with circles and other basic shapes.

Now add smaller details, such as the chin and the feet. Here, small circles are used for feet, eyes, and chin.

Last of all, rub out any lines you don't want, and color your picture in, adding tiny details like whiskers and claws.

Sleepy Lidded eyes and open mouth, yawning, look sleepy

Sad Eyes drooping down at the corner look sad

Startled Round eyes, raised eyebrows, and round mouth look scared

Angry V-shaped eyebrows and mouth turned down at corners look angry

Patch says… Felt pen is good for cartoons because it gives a simple, bold outline. The colors in cartoons are usually quite strong, too, so felt pen is also good for filling in.

Scared cat: round, popping eyes, drops of sweat

Frightened horse: round eyes, sweat drops

Wriggling lizard: little lines around feet and tail show movement

Goody-goody parrot: with halo above head

Thinking mouse: round eyes, straight mouth, tapping fingers

Worried fish: round eyes, mouth turned down

Dizzy cat: ring of stars, heavy lids, silly smile

Watching monkey: pupils in corner of eyes, small smile

Greedy mouse: tongue licking lips

75

Moving animals

Drawing moving animals is very hard, but the more you practice, the easier it will get. Because it is so difficult to tell what is happening by watching a live animal move, you need to learn about movement by studying and copying pictures of moving animals. Look in magazines, newspapers, or books. If you can take photographs of a cat or dog running, a rabbit hopping, or a budgie flying, that would be even better.

On these pages are pictures of all kinds of creatures moving, which you can copy. Each sequence is broken down into separate stages to show the movement. You can add your own pet's features and colors afterward.

When you have learned more about how an animal's body works, you can try drawing from life. If there are parts you are not sure about, you can always check back to the pictures you looked at and copied. Remember that it is easier to draw your pet from the side than from the front.

You will need to draw very quickly, so choose a drawing material that covers the paper quickly. Pencil is rather slow, but charcoal, soft chalk, or wax crayon would be good. Using the side to draw with, rather than the tip, is even quicker.

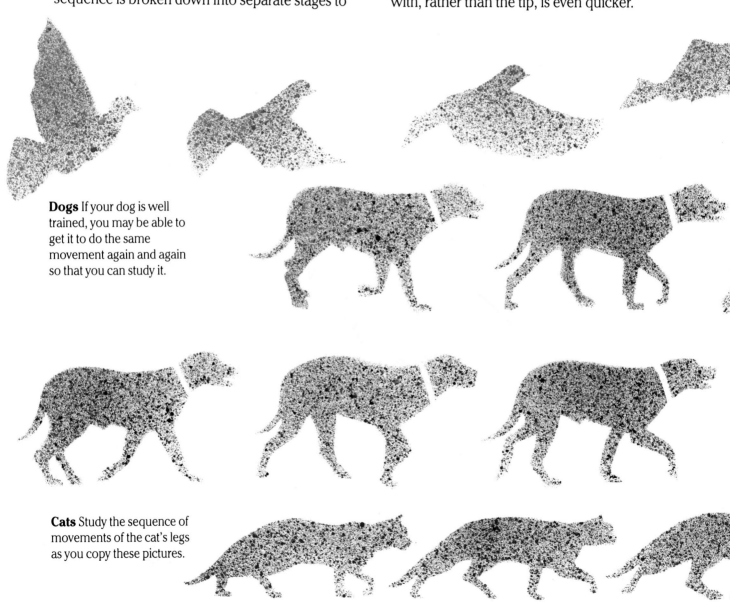

Dogs If your dog is well trained, you may be able to get it to do the same movement again and again so that you can study it.

Cats Study the sequence of movements of the cat's legs as you copy these pictures.

76

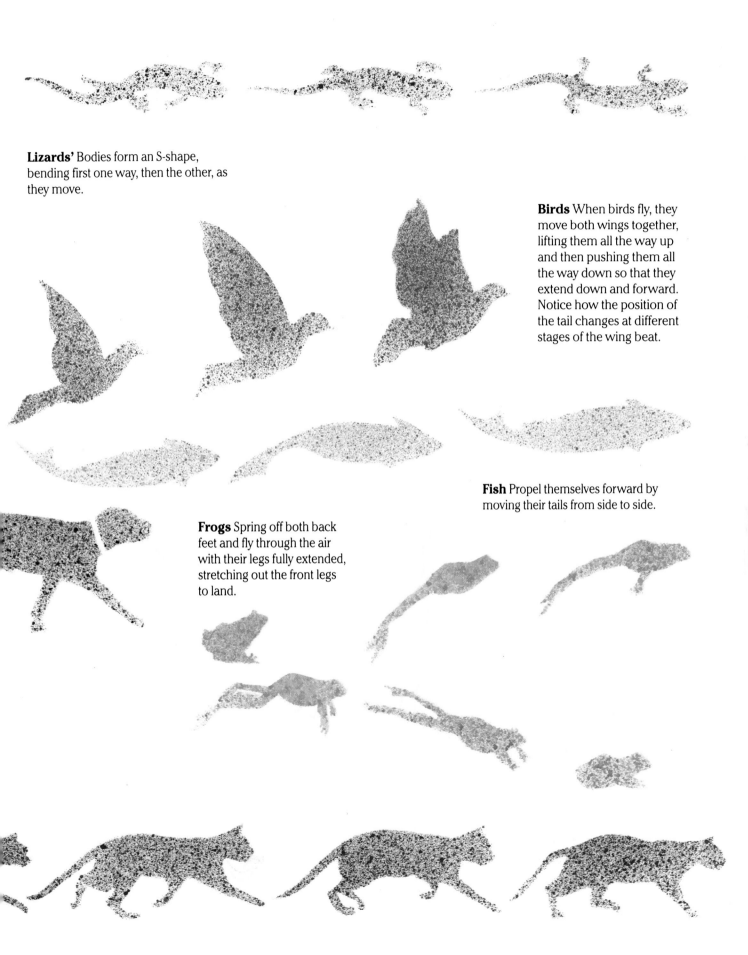

Lizards' Bodies form an S-shape, bending first one way, then the other, as they move.

Birds When birds fly, they move both wings together, lifting them all the way up and then pushing them all the way down so that they extend down and forward. Notice how the position of the tail changes at different stages of the wing beat.

Fish Propel themselves forward by moving their tails from side to side.

Frogs Spring off both back feet and fly through the air with their legs fully extended, stretching out the front legs to land.

Horses See how the horse picks up one foot at a time as it walks. A horse moves differently when it is trotting, cantering, and galloping. When it jumps, it takes off from both hind feet together, but it lands on one front foot followed by the other.

Dog running At the start of the stride, with its feet gathered under it, its body is compressed. In the middle of the stride it is at full stretch.

Cat running Even at full speed, the cat always has one foot on the ground.

Flicker book

When you see a movie or cartoon, it seems as if you are watching one long moving picture. In fact, movies and cartoons just trick you into thinking this. They are actually a sequence of lots and lots of *separate* pictures that flash past your eyes so fast that they seem to blend into one movement.

Although it takes a very long time to make a movie or cartoon, you can still use the same basic idea, in a much simpler way, to make a *flicker book* of your pet. When you flick through the book, you will see your pet "move."

Choose some simple activity, such as your horse jumping a fence, or your budgie landing on its perch. Think of all the different movements that go into doing this one thing. Do some rough sketches first to try out your idea.

You could look back to pages 76 to 79, which are all about moving animals.

You will need
- sheets of paper
- something to draw with (pen, pencil, etc)
- stapler, or needle and thread
- scissors

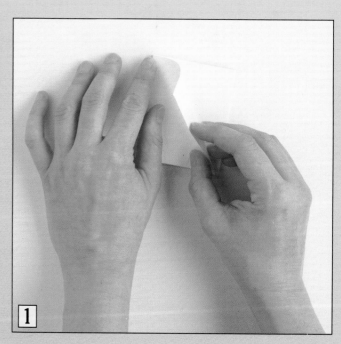

1

Cut out some strips of paper, all the same size (you can always cut out more later if you find you haven't enough). Fold them in half down the middle.

80

Here are some flicker-book ideas based on the sequences of moving animals on pages 76 to 79.

An animal can be made to look as if it is moving by changing its position in relation to another object.

If there is too much of a difference between one picture and the next, it will create a "jump" in the sequence, making it seem jerky when you flick through it. You will need to add some extra pictures between the ones where the sequence jumps.

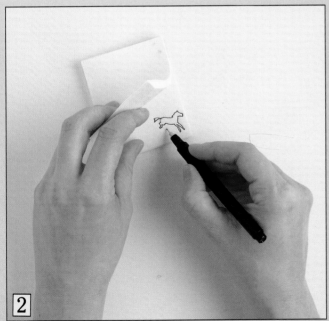

2

Staple or sew the strips together to make a book.

Start at the back of the book. On the right-hand side of each strip of paper,

3

do a drawing of each movement in your sequence.

Flick through the book, from back to front, and watch your pet "move."

Texture

Texture is the name for how something feels when you touch it. Texture is an important part of how your pet looks – for example, a cat with a short, sleek coat will look different from a cat with long, soft, fluffy fur. They are both cats but the texture of their coats makes them look different.

Showing the texture of your pet's coat will add something extra to your picture, and make it look more lifelike. You can show different textures by using different materials. For example, smudged pastel or charcoal would be good for a fluffy cat, and smooth, even paint or felt pen could be used for the sleek, shorthaired cat. The examples shown here will give you some more ideas, but try thinking up some of your own, too. Think also about how to do different parts of your pet – would you use the same material for all of them? For example, would you do a smooth, wet nose in the same way as a rough, shaggy coat?

Always be sensitive to texture. It's as important a part of your picture as getting your pet's shape right.

Fluffy cat Colored pastels in four different browns have been smudged together here to give a soft, fluffy look.

Scaly lizard Beautiful paint colors have been worked over with criss-cross pen lines to show the scaly "feel" of this lizard's skin.

Shiny fish The smooth, shiny skin of this fish has been painted a smooth, even orange, with touches of white paint added for highlights.

Shaggy mouse Colored pen lines look like coarse hair on this mouse. Its smooth ears and tail have been painted.

Velvety rabbit Soft black and brown oil pastel give this rabbit its velvety-smooth coat.

Feathery bird Lots of colored pencil lines give the soft look of feathers.

Shaggy dog Scribbled colored pencil in black and gray shows this dog's rough, curly coat.

Pictures from rubbings

Have you ever done a pencil or crayon rubbing? Perhaps you have done one using a coin, and watched the pattern of the coin begin to appear on the paper.

To do any rubbing, you need something with a rough surface that you can feel with your fingers, such as corrugated cardboard, sandpaper, or even wood. If the surface is too smooth, you will just get a solid area of color, without any pattern.

The ladybug rubbing shown here uses the same template over and over again. This kind of rubbing is good if you have a lot of pets of one kind – a tankful of goldfish or a box of ladybugs. Instead of drawing or painting each one separately, you simply cut out a template and move it around under your paper, taking a rubbing each time.

You can fix the shape in place to stop it moving. And remember not to use thick paper, or you won't be able to "pick up" the shape underneath.

You will need

- drawing paper or thin cardboard for cutting out the ladybug shape
- pencil
- eraser
- scissors
- paper punch
- paper
- crayons

Rubbings using a template Draw the shape of your pet, keeping it simple. Simple silhouettes work best, and are easier to cut out. For the ladybugs just draw the body shape – details like legs can be added later.

Cut out the shape you have drawn. For spots or eyes, cut holes in the shape, or punch them out with a paper punch.

Lay the shape on a tray or board, sticking it in position if you like. Lay the paper over the top. Rub over the shape with

Experimenting with rubbings

You can take rubbings from all kinds of things, but for a picture of your pet you need to use something that will give the right kind of texture – so try out different things first. Corrugated cardboard was used for the dog's shaggy coat (below); for the snail (right) a wicker tablemat was used; and the parrot was made by rubbing crayon on paper laid over a tablemat and textured wallpaper.

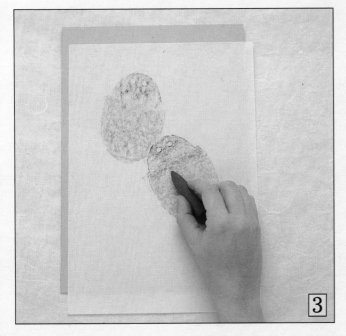

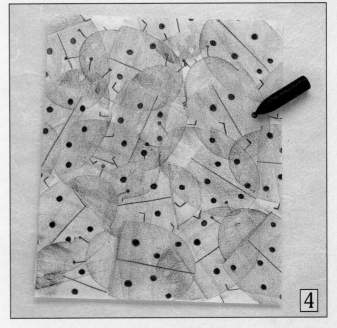

the side of your crayon. Move the shape to another place and repeat, until your paper is covered with rubbings. Let the rubbings overlap – it will make the picture more interesting.

Now use your crayons to add any details you want, such as spots, antennae, and legs, or any extra colors. This is a good way to produce a really busy design.

Measuring and Proportions

Often, people draw things the size they imagine they are, rather than looking very carefully and drawing them the size they actually look. If you want to do a really good picture of your pet, it's very important to get the *proportions* right – this means getting the sizes of the different parts right for each other. It's no good drawing a beautiful head for your budgie, for example, if it's too big or too small for the body.

A good way to get proportions right is by measuring. You may find it difficult at first, but it gets easier with practice.

Hold your pencil up in front of your pet, and use your thumb to measure the different parts of the animal, as in the picture below. Then make marks on the paper to show how long or wide each part is. You may discover that your pet's body is three times as long as its head, or twice as wide. Using these marks as a guide, do your drawing over them.

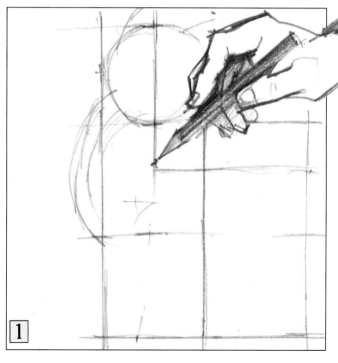

Enlarging a picture
It is possible to make a copy larger (or smaller) than the original picture or photograph. Trace the outline of the picture on to tracing paper. Now divide the tracing evenly into squares, using a ruler to measure the squares.

To measure your pet, hold your pencil up, the top level with the top of its head, and "mark" its chin with your thumb.

Measure down the body to see how many head-sizes you can fit in. Make marks down the paper to show how many "heads" you measured. Work out the width in the same way.

[2]

On your paper, mark the size you want your copy to be, then divide it into the same number of squares as on the tracing. Copy the little bit of outline that appears in each square, joining up the lines as you go so that you get a complete outline.

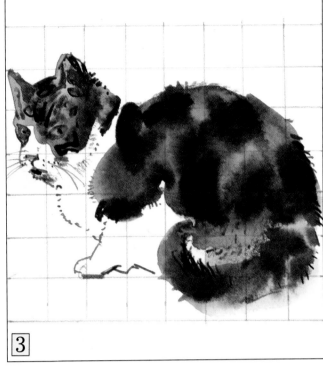

[3]

Now you can fill in all the smaller details, such as the whiskers. Using the original picture as your guide, paint or color in your outline. And don't forget to rub out the little squares!

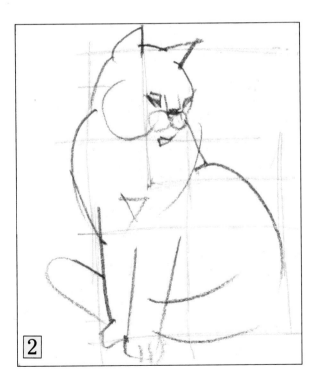

[2]

Using the measurements you have made on the paper to guide you, start drawing in the outline of your pet. When you are happy with the outline, rub out the measurements, and fill in the details.

[3]

Here is the finished picture.

Making the picture work

Composition is the name for how you arrange the things in your picture. Here are some hints on how to create a good composition.

One of the basic rules of composition is to have something in the "foreground" (front), something in the "middle ground" (middle), and something in the "background" (back). This will give your picture depth, and make it seem as if you are looking right into the scene in front of you. Think of it as being like one of those puppet theaters made of cardboard: the characters stand at the front, the wings on to the stage are behind them, and the painted scenery is right at the back.

Besides thinking about where to place the objects in your picture, you can make your composition work even better by careful choice of size and color. The picture opposite shows how important these are.

Inventing a framework Imagine your picture divided up by a framework of lines, with each of the important things in the picture placed along one of the lines. You could even draw the lines on your paper, but don't place them across the center – your composition will look much better if the lines are above or below the middle, or to one side of center.

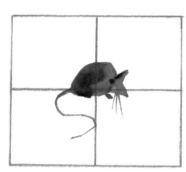

Poor composition: lines cut across center.

Good composition: lines to one side of center.

Choosing a shape for your picture

There are two basic shapes for pictures: "portrait," which is tall and high, and "horizontal," which is long and wide. The picture above is a horizontal shape, and the picture on the left is a portrait shape. In the horizontal picture above, you can see all of the horse's head, but a portrait shape "matches" the shape of his head better.

To show all of the snake in the picture above, a long, horizontal shape has been chosen. But sometimes leaving out part of the animal can make a more dramatic picture. In the portrait-shaped picture on the left, the artist was only interested in the snake's head. The portrait shape also suits the L-shaped outline of the snake.

your composition will look better if you arrange things in groups, rather than place them on their own

objects look larger in the front, and gradually become smaller as they get farther away

more detail also makes things look closer; the farther away they are, the less detail you can see

overlapping parts of your drawing gives depth

warm, strong colors, such as reds or deep browns, make things look closer;

paler, cool colors look farther away

Rabbit in a hutch

Why not make a picture of your pet in its home? This picture of a rabbit in its hutch uses a variety of materials and involves painting a picture of the rabbit, cutting out the hutch in cardboard, and then gluing the hutch over the picture of the rabbit. String is used to make the hutch door.

See what other ways you can think of for painting pets in the places where they live. For example, you could do a pony in its stable by cutting out the stable in cardboard, and then cutting the top half of the door around three sides so that it opens. Make a painting of the pony's head and stick it to the back of the stable so that the pony's head is in the open door. The pictures opposite should also help to give you some ideas.

You will need

- sheet of paper
- piece of thin, colored cardboard
- paints
- pencil
- brush
- scissors
- glue
- tape
- string

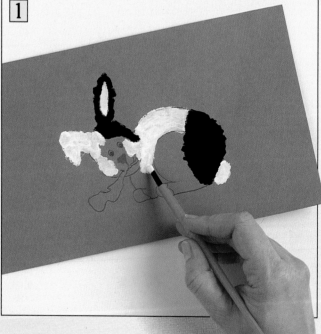

1

Draw a picture of a rabbit in the center of a large piece of paper, and paint it in.

2

Cut out the hutch shape in thin cardboard, and cut out the door in the front of the hutch. The hutch must be the right size for your rabbit.

For a picture of goldfish in their bowl, you could cut out a frame in the shape of the bowl, and stick clear plastic wrap across the back of the frame to give an impression of glass. Then stick the frame down over the picture of the fish. The fish, plants and rocks have been colored with felt-tip pen, and the water lightly shaded in with blue crayon.

When painting a bird in its cage, remember that the bars need to be drawn over the top of the bird to give the idea that it is in its cage. The cage bars were drawn in with light grey felt-tip pen.

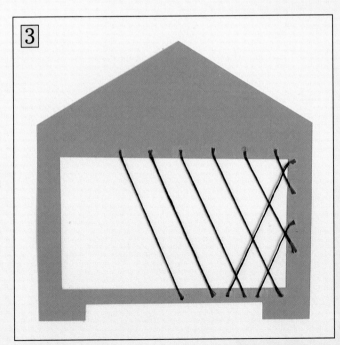

Glue or tape pieces of string on the back of the hutch in a diagonal pattern across the hutch door.

Cover the back of the hutch with glue and stick it down over your picture of the rabbit.

Out and about

Most animals like to go outside and enjoy the sunshine and fresh air. Does your pet have a favorite spot outdoors? Perhaps it likes to keep cool in the shade of a tree, or does it prefer to bask in the sun on the doorstep or window sill? All dogs love going for walks – in the park, in the fields, or in the woods, depending on where you live. If they get the chance, they also love to play about in water, at the beach or by the river.

Think about what your pet likes to do best when it is outside, and do a picture of it, using whatever materials you like. You could draw your pet close up, or farther away as part of a more general scene.

When you are doing this kind of picture, it will be helpful to look back at some of the other pages earlier in the book. For example, you may need to check back to see how to draw moving animals, on pages 76 to 79. Getting a good composition (pages 88 to 89) is also important here.

Making a viewfinder When you are looking at a scene in front of you, it can be difficult to decide which parts of it to include in your picture, and what to put where. Should your pet be big or small, for example, and should it be at the top, bottom, or side of the picture? This is where a *viewfinder* can help.

You can make one yourself out of cardboard. Cut a square or rectangle out of a piece of cardboard (or a circle if you want a round picture). The cut-out shape should be the same shape as your finished picture, but need not be the same size.

Hold the viewfinder up in front of you to "frame" what you see. Move it about until you find what looks best. If you want your pet to be big, go closer to it; if you want it to be smaller, go further away.

And now – before you forget – quickly sketch the view you have chosen on paper.

By cropping the picture on the left of the dog, a strong composition has been achieved in which the dog and the wood pile balance each other.

Patch says… When you are doing a picture of an outdoor scene, mix your colors carefully. The colors in nature are much softer and subtler than those that come straight from a tube or jar!

"Close-up" pictures The dog in the picture on the opposite page is out in the country, and is seen from quite a distance. If you are doing a picture of your pet at home, it will probably be much closer to you – lying on a wall in the sun, or hiding in a bed of flowers.

To make your pet look "close-up," you should let it take up more of the space in the picture. In this picture, the cat almost fills the area, and the things around it are not important. In the opposite picture, the dog is part of the whole landscape.

Collage cat If you are doing a picture of your pet outdoors, you don't need to stick just to paint or pencils. Why not use collage as well? It could save you a lot of work. Instead of having to paint each flower or leaf, or even the bricks in a brick wall, you could just cut out and paste down pictures of them. Experiment with making your own collage bits and pieces. A collage of pasted leaf shapes, cut from tracing paper scribbled with green pencil, can look very effective.

To: Michelle

from Mommy